THE STUDENT LOAN HANDBOOK

Lana J. Chandler
& Michael D. Boggs

BETTERWAY PUBLICATIONS, INC.
WHITE HALL, VIRGINIA

Published by Betterway Publications, Inc.
Box 82
White Hall, VA 22987

Cover design by Deborah B. Chappel
Typography by East Coast Typography, Inc.

Library of Congress Cataloging-in-Publication Data

Chandler, Lana J.
    The student loan handbook: all about the guaranteed student loan program and other forms of financial aid/Lana J. Chandler and Michael D. Boggs
        p.   cm.
    Bibliography: p.
    Includes indes.
    Summary: Describes all popular forms of financial aid for college, trade school, or technical training, including work study, grant, and scholarship programs, and presents family financial planning guidelines.
    ISBN 0-932620-82-5 (pbk.): $7.95
    1. Student loan funds—United States—Handbooks, manuals, etc.
2. Student aid—United States—Handbooks, manuals, etc. [1. Student aid. 2. Student loan funds. 3. Scholarships. 4. Universities and colleges—Finance.]   I. Boggs, Michael D., 1948-   . II. Title.
LB2340.2.C42 1987   87-15918
378′.362′0973—dc19   · CIP
                                                                       AC

Printed in the United States of America
0987654321

To my wife Sandra
whose patience and perseverance was a quiet
encouragement to complete this work.
To Nicole and Jodi, my daughters.
To John K. Fischer
whose support made this work possible.
Mike

To Jean Smith O'Connor
for always believing in me.
Lana

Contents

PART 3: OTHER FORMS OF FINANCIAL AID

PART 4: FINANCIAL PLANNING

APPENDICES

Introduction

Getting a postsecondary education is not an impossible dream. Almost everyone who wants to go to college can.

With today's soaring costs of higher education, this opening statement may seem a little too optimistic. It takes a lot of money these days just to eat, keep a roof over your head and pay the bills. Nevertheless, it really is possible to pay for a higher education — the education you want! All it takes is discovering what's available in Student Financial Aid and learning how to take advantage of it.

More than 12 million students are currently attending some type of postsecondary school. These schools include colleges and universities, trade and technical schools and business schools. Twice as many American as Soviet citizens are enrolled in educational programs beyond high school. We have 10 times as many students as France and 15 times the total student enrollment of the United Kingdom. Do you believe that all of these people are wealthy enough to pay for education without having to depend on some form of student financial aid?

If you do, then it's time to look at some of the financial realities of our educational system. Most postsecondary schools aren't cheap. To compound the problem, most families don't have enough money to meet these costs. So what's the solution?

Financial aid. In 1987, the United States will spend an estimated $261 billion on education. More than $11.9 billion of this sizable sum will be spent on federal financial assistance to students. It's just one more way America is investing in her people.

Some aid programs sponsored by the federal government are grants. If you receive a grant, you don't have to pay it back. The Pell Grant and Supplemental Education Opportunity Grant (SEOG) programs are the "big two".

Low-interest loans are available through other programs sponsored by the federal government. If you receive one of these loans, it must eventually be repaid in full (principal plus interest.) The Guaranteed Student Loan Program (GSLP) is one of the most popular programs of this type. In fact, we have devoted one entire section of our guide to the GSLP and related programs, Parent Loans for Undergraduate Students (PLUS) and Supplemental Loans for Students (SLS).

Other forms of federal aid are typically categorized as "campus-based programs". The school's financial aid administrator is responsible for distributing these monies. The National Direct Student Loan (NSDL), now known as the Perkins Loan Program and the College Work Study (CWS) program, are examples of these campus-based programs.

Numerous other money sources are also worth exploring. Since a postsecondary education seems to cost more each year, it's wise to learn about as many sources of funds as possible.

If you're working for a company, your employer may offer tuition reimbursement for certain courses. Your parents' workplace may be another source of aid. Labor unions and corporations are both sources for scholarships. They may also support low-interest loans for employees or members of the employees' family. Foundations, religious organizations, fraternities, sororities, clubs, community organizations and civic groups are staunch supporters of scholarship funds. Check with your public library for information on state and private sources of aid.

It's important to realize financial need isn't always the only consideration. Athletic ability, academic excellence, musical talent or an interest in the health professions are all qualifying conditions when it comes to financial aid. Organizations connected with your particular field of interest often support higher education assistance programs. Good examples are the American Medical Association and the America Bar Association. The U.S. Department of Labor's *Occupational Outlook Handbook* is a good reference to check for potential sources of aid. If you have been in the military, investigate Veteran benefits. Your local Veterans Administration Office can help you.

Contact your state's student assistance agency for information about state aid. Every state has its own name for such a program and differs in amount, eligibility criteria and application procedure. Contact the financial aid administrator at each school in which you are interested to find out which programs are applicable to that institution. Your high school counselor can help locate the schools that specialize in the education you want.

In other words, do your homework when it's time to finance an education.

Federal programs based on financial need are the primary topics covered in this guide. Since more students have financial need in common than any other eligibility requirement, we chose to concentrate on such programs. We hope that our information will help make you more aware of what's available. At least you'll be better prepared to discuss student aid with your high school counselor or financial aid administrator. But most important of all, we want you to realize that financing your education can be easy. Education is a remarkably important investment in yourself and our country, so go for it! The money is there, all it takes is discovering how to find it.

Several programs presented here are "need-based". This means that your family's individual financial situation is analyzed in order to determine your own unique level of aid. Case studies are utilized in several sections, and we will describe several "typical" families in different sections of this book. In order to depict as broad an example as possible, we will make generalizations about several family situations. Review these case studies and compare them with your own family. We realize that there are numerous variables — family size, income, assets, place of residence and local economy — that will have a bearing on the true eligibility for financial aid. Don't be disappointed if the "typical" family presented is not the same as your own.

Our examples will include families with one, two or three children. Some families may have more than one child seeking postsecondary education, while others will have a parent as well as a child in college or other postsecondary programs. We will examine how retirement or status as a single parent affects the eligibility. Remember that the need-based aid process holds unique results for each individual applicant. We urge you to ask your high school counselor, banker or financial aid officer to conduct a review of your individual needs qualifications. This can be done well before a student becomes a candidate for a program of postsecondary education. The results will help you to begin the planning and application stage for financial aid.

Chapter 1

What is the GSLP?

Earning a college education is a part of the great American dream for millions of young people. Over half of today's high school graduates choose to pursue a postsecondary education. In 1985 approximately 12.2 million students were enrolled in postsecondary education programs. The total cost of their education approached $55 billion, and this figure means that each student averaged about $4,500 for just one year of school.

A college education is no longer associated with social class, race or the family's income bracket. An increasing number of young people see their educational goals as ways to better their lives . They know that a good education is one of the surest means of achieving a more prosperous future.

The word "prosperous" doesn't mean rich. It means successful. Perhaps your goal is to be a social worker. You probably won't make a fortune, but then again that may not be what you're striving for. However, to fulfill this dream requires a college education. In fact, the cold reality is that most jobs in the United States today require college or postsecondary training.

What is Really Happening in the 1980's

First, more people want a postsecondary education. Next, although enrollment in our high schools has been steadily declining, schools and colleges have been unable to reduce costs in order to make education available to a wider segment of the public. Last, financial aid is playing a larger role than ever in helping people meet educational goals. Nearly 75 percent of students in postsecondary programs now receive some form of financial aid.

Since 1981, the cost of a postsecondary education has increased at almost twice the rate of inflation. Not only has the demand for a postsecondary education soared, but so has its cost. Family circumstances, such as divorce, leave many of today's students with very limited budgets. Add in the threat of returning inflation and sluggish economic conditions, and we can see why many despair.

The United States has millions of young people eager for a postsecondary education who cannot afford the associated expenses. The Guaranteed Student Loan Program, more commonly known as the GSLP, is a popular solution more students are discovering each year.

Most people start a business by borrowing money. It's an investment in themselves and their ideas. A postsecondary education is also an investment. You are investing in yourself to achieve better earning power and a more rewarding career. Acquiring the skills and resources necessary to fulfill job ambitions more often than not takes money. Since a businessman borrows capital to develop investments, isn't it just as practical for students to borrow necessary funds when investing in the education of their choice?

The United States Congress felt that students needed a way to borrow money for an education. Unlike the businessman we described earlier, students rarely have collateral or credit history. Congress recognized these special circumstances and created the GSLP in 1965 under the Higher Education Act (HEA).

The intent of the GSLP was to help students from lower- and middle-income families finance a postsecondary education by taking out low-interest loans in their own names. When first introduced in 1965, the interest rate on a GSL was six percent. Congress further defined the maximum amount an individual could borrow each year, as well as a maximum for all federal student loan monies owed by an individual.

Between 1965 and 1978, Congress amended the GSLP on more than a half dozen occasions. A "special allowance" was established for lenders. Eligibility requirements were revised, taking into consideration a student's true financial need. Interest rates have been modified over the years, along with maximum amounts. The Student Loan Marketing Association (Sallie Mae) was created; the latter serves as a secondary market and warehousing facility for GSL's. In October 1986, President Reagan signed new legislation which renews the Higher Education Amendments for another five years and makes significant changes in rules, borrowing limits and eligibility.

Throughout these legislative changes, however, the GSLP's

purpose has remained the same. It provides students with low-interest loans in order to help meet the costs of attending colleges, universities, vocational and technical schools. Under the GSLP, money is borrowed without the benefit of collateral or an established credit history. Lenders are willing to make such loans because the federal government guarantees them against borrower default, death, disability or bankruptcy. It is mostly students, not parents, who take out GSLs. There are additional loan plans through the GSLP that are designed for the parent and independent student borrower. We'll talk about these plans more later in this book.

One very attractive point about student loans is that the government pays the interest due on the loan so long as the student remains in school half-time and makes satisfactory progress. If the parent or student takes out an independent loan, however, the government does not pay the interest.

Today the GSLP is our nation's major source of credit for education loans. Congress has succeeded in creating a partnership between the federal government, community lenders and private loan guarantee agencies in order to benefit students. Because of the GSLP, lenders are encouraged to grant low-interest loans to students. In 1985, approximately 29 percent of those pursuing a postsecondary education used the GSLP in order to obtain necessary funds. Nearly 13,000 lending institutions participated in granting loans to these students.

Who Administers the GSLP?

It is primarily administered by state and private "guarantee agencies". The latter are non-profit institutions. Guarantee agencies serve as intermediate loan insurers, defaulted loan collectors and administrative processors for the United States Department of Education. We'll talk more about the role of guarantee agencies later in this chapter.

Who Benefits From the GSLP?

Millions of students and their families benefit from the GSLP when faced with the financial realities of a postsecondary education. In fact, these programs really consist of two components:

1. Student Loans
2. Parent Loans

Although their purposes are the same, these loan programs vary in such aspects as eligibility requirements, repayment terms, dependency tests, etc. Later in this book we'll discuss each type of loan in detail.

Approximately 8,000 domestic institutions qualify for participation in the GSLP. These schools must have obtained certification by the Division of Eligibility and Agency Evaluation of the Office of Education. In addition they must agree with the rules set forth by the Commissioner of the U.S. Office of Education.

Of the total number, 3,750 are two- and four-year traditional, degree-granting institutions. An estimated 4,250 are vocational, technical, nursing and other non-degree granting institutions.

Foreign schools may also be eligible for GSLP support. However, they must follow the same rules as schools in the United States. Furthermore, such schools must enter into an agreement with the Department of Education's commissioner. As of September 1985, approximately 575 foreign schools in 49 countries have signed participation agreements with the Department of Education.

Now let's take a look at the costs and repayment terms associated with a GSL.

Naturally if you borrow money, you must eventually pay it back. Along with principal, (the amount actually borrowed) you will owe interest. Depending on WHEN you took out a GSL, the interest rate may be seven, eight or nine percent. Students currently taking out a GSL for the first time are charged eight percent interest for the first through fourth years of repayment, then the rate increases to 10 percent for the remaining years. (See Chapter 7 — How Repayment Works for more information.)

Remember that these interest charges begin ONLY after you've left school, dropped below half-time status, or fail to make satisfactory progress. An even more attractive bonus feature of a GSL is that you're granted an additional six-month grace period, interest free, before payments must begin. That gives you time to find a job and adjust to life outside of school.

In addition to interest, a student borrower must pay a one-time guarantee fee. This is deducted from the proceeds of the loan. This fee can be up to three percent per year of the projected principal amount of the loan, based on the anticipated school period, plus the grace period. The fee is then forwarded by the lender to the guarantor in return for assurance that the loan will be paid in full.

A one-time origination fee is also assessed. In the past, this fee has been 5.0 to 5.5 percent of the total loan. The federal government passes this origination fee on to the lender. These fees help to reduce the government's cost of subsidizing these low-interest loans. They also compensate the lender for the time and expenses associated with processing the applications and disbursing the loan proceeds.

TYPICAL MONTHLY REPAYMENT
(For five- to 10-year periods at eight percent interest)

Amount Borrowed	Monthly Payment	Years to Repay
$ 2,500	$ 50.70	5
5,000	60.75	10
7,500	90.97	10
10,000	121.30	10
12,500	151.62	10
15,000	181.95	10
20,000	242.60	10
25,000	303.25	10

Note: Rates of interest are scheduled to climb to 10 percent in the fifth year of repayment. This will increase the payment amount shown here.

The repayment period, at the borrower's option, may span 10 years in length. However, the lender and borrower may agree to slightly longer repayment periods to avoid undue financial hardship on the borrower.

When establishing repayment schedules, there is one condition. A minimum monthly payment of $50 is mandatory. This $50 payment covers both principal and interest. Because of this minimum requirement, small loans will be repaid in a shorter period of time.

The costs associated with a GSL, as well as repayment terms, are established by Congress, but Congress changes such requirements from time to time. However, if you already have a student loan, it is doubtful that any new legislation will affect it. Past policies, too, have allowed all borrowings to remain at the rates in effect when the first loan was obtained, in spite of subsequent Congressional changes.

The term "guarantee agencies" has been used several times. It's important that you understand exactly what is meant by this particular term, since it will continue to appear throughout this publication.

Guarantee agencies play a vital role in the GSLP's success. Banks, savings & loans, credit unions and other financial institutions feel safe making student loans because Congress has guaranteed that such loans will be repaid. If the borrower fails to pay back the lender, the guarantee agency reimburses the lender; then the government, through the Department of Education, reimburses the guarantee agency for part of their expense. This is called "re-insurance".

The amount refunded to the guarantee agency depends on the agency's success in collecting the defaulted loans acquired from the lender during the claim procedure. The guarantee agency assists the lender in administrative functions, reporting and claims collections. This helps the lender and the school. A well-run program ultimately helps the student borrower by ensuring that there are interested businesses involved in making loan funds available.

The Higher Education Assistance Foundation (HEAF) and United Student Aid Fund (USAF) are private, non-profit corporations. Their business is to guarantee student loans. HEAF is our nation's largest, private non-profit guarantor, insuring loans for students attending postsecondary institutions in every state. Through more than 2,000 lenders, HEAF has guaranteed more than 2 million loans to students and their families.

The state where you live may also have its own state-sponsored guarantee program. These State Guarantee Agencies (SGA's) have been established for the purposes of guaranteeing student loans and providing such related services as collecting payments on defaulted loans. Their policies and requirements are similar to those of the private non-profit guarantor. State agencies are funded by their respective state government and, like private agencies, are re-insured by the Department of Education.

Along with SGA's, many states have also established related but separate State Student Loan Agencies. These agencies are sources of loan funds when funds aren't available through commercial sources. Because of such agencies, students and their families may find last resort sources of student loans.

Lenders may not always have sufficient funds available to meet loan demand. Remember that private lenders (i.e. commercial banks) are not required by law to make student loans nor are they required, if they do make them, to set aside any specific amount of funds for the program. Funds available for loans must be divided among requests for automobiles, homes and businesses as well as students seeking financial aid. Sometimes there just isn't enough money to go around!

If your loan is insured by an SGA, the latter may also charge you an insurance premium. The amount charged varies from state to state. However, in no event can the premium equal more than three percent per year of the loan's outstanding principal balance. The fees are usually collected when disbursed.

One of the best ways to summarize the role of the guarantee agency is to say that it promotes good lender participation. By insuring the lender against borrower default, more lenders are encouraged to participate in the GSLP. More participation by lenders, in turn, means better opportunities for students to pursue higher education goals.

Chapter 2

How Much and When to Borrow

If the GSLP is your solution to meeting college expenses, don't forget to recognize the importance of timing—when to apply for the loan. For probably the first time in your life, you are personally handling a major financial transaction. Keep in mind, therefore, that a GSL isn't something that can be hastily arranged. Like most business transactions, a GSL takes time to travel through the appropriate channels.

Get your finances in order well before the school term starts and apply for financial aid early. You can complete a financial aid form or similar application through the College Scholarship Service (CSS) or the American College Testing Service (ACT) and receive an analysis of your family's "expected family contribution". This contribution is the extent of financial support your family is expected to pay toward your education. (We will discuss the meaning and impact of family contributions more in a later chapter).

How much will you be able to borrow? The family contribution has a direct impact on this figure. But you need to consider just what expenses are eligible to be funded with the proceeds of a GSL. You will see "college costs, student budget, loan budget" and "costs of attendance" figures interchanged. They are not the same as "tuition" or "tuition and fees" that you see in most college catalogues. The following list of categories and items are those that make up the "college budget":

> Tuition & Fees
> +Books and Supplies
> +Housing
> +Meals
> +Personal Expenses
> +Transportation
> ———————————
> =College Budget

Numerous factors influence the total cost of a postsecondary education. A college may have 12 to 18 (or even more) different budgets that apply to different student "statuses". Rarely do any two colleges charge the same for all expenses. Housing may be higher at one, while tuition is less. The program you select also affects the total costs. For example, a science major must purchase more lab equipment than an accounting major. Will you be a commuting or resident student? Commuters typically save when it comes to housing and meals. That's one of the reasons why many choose to attend a school in their own community.

The School Budget process includes two steps. First, certain costs are fixed and direct—tuition and fees and books and supplies (which vary by program or major). Second, some costs are more indirect and variable. Housing, meals, transportation and personal expenses have the greatest variance. The budget-making process includes consideration of the on-campus costs of living and off-campus housing, transportation and other necessary expenses. These costs are usually determined by studying and surveying the housing and other costs in the immediate community surrounding the school. To these costs, adjustments must be made to compensate for married students' expense allowance and the availability of and costs of public and private transportation. As you can see, this is a very difficult and detailed process.

In the final analysis, the college will also price its respective budget for items such as housing, meals and transportation may not accurately reflect the actual costs in the area. But your individual tastes vary too. It's safe to assume that the budget is just a guide to the total expected costs, but an important guide nonetheless.

When to Apply

This time of your life is one of the most important. Decisions made now have a direct bearing on your future career and earnings. To repeat an old cliche: "Don't wait until the last minute". This could never be more true, but there are limitations on just when you can take actual steps toward the application process.

Limitation #1: You cannot apply for a GSL until you have been accepted, enrolled or about to enroll in the school. Many students receive their acceptances well before graduating from high school. That's fine and the time until school begins can be used to continue to "pin down" aid and loans.

Limitation #2: The school or college needs-analysis service (ACT or CSS mentioned earlier) cannot usually complete an analysis of your family finances until they have actual or accurate estimates of your family's income, income tax, etc. for the calendar or tax year PRECEDING the year of admission to school. You simply may not have the necessary data to make a good judgment of loan eligibility until early in the year that you expect to begin school.

What are we saying? Apply early, but you can't? No, you can take steps to get a head start. One step would be asking your school counselor if he or she has the ability to calculate your family's expected contribution based on the most recently available financial information. Even if this is years before you expect to enter school, the results may give you a guide of what to expect and may suggest other steps to take. Many high school and junior high school counselors have tables or personal computer programs that can calculate estimates for you.

Depending on who guarantees your loan, your approval varies after the application is complete. Obviously the late summer and fall is the busiest time for the schools, lenders, and guarantee agencies. Please allow ample time for the approvals. Apply as early as the school will accept your application. In general, your approval and guarantee takes no longer than 30 days if everything is in order.

It's comforting to know as early as possible what you are getting. Remember, however, that the loan funds will not be sent to you for your immediate use. Loan checks are either sent directly to the school or are made payable to the student and school jointly, and sent to the student. In either case, you won't be able to use the funds until you are at the school finalizing your registration.

Chapter 3

The Student Loan

Student loans are made to students. They are not made to parents or legal guardians. That doesn't mean that you have to be of high school age in order to qualify for a GSL. What it does mean is that you must qualify as a student, and students can be any age.

As a student applying for a GSL, you are personally assuming responsibility for this debt. It becomes your obligation to pay it back. In fact, if you are coming straight out of high school, then more than likely a student loan also represents the beginning of your credit history. When the time comes to begin repayment of this loan, be a responsible borrower. Failure to repay this debt can make other lenders hesitant to deal with you on car loans, credit cards, personal loans for vacations, furniture, etc.

Can Anyone Take Out a GSL?

No. Potential borrowers must meet certain eligibility requirements. To qualify for a GSL you must:

1. Be a United States citizen, national or registered alien.

2. Be enrolled at least half-time in an eligible program at a school participating in the U.S. Department of Education's financial aid program.

3. Be making satisfactory progress as determined by the school.

4. Be within the dollar limitations of the GSLP.

5. Be free from default on any student financial aid program.

6. Have signed a Statement of Registration Status indication that you have registered with the Selective Service, if you are required to do so. This requirement applies to males at least 18 years of age, who are citizens or eligible non-citizens and are not currently on active duty in the Armed

Forces. To ensure that students comply with this requirement, the Department of Education will select a sample of students and verify their registration status with the Selective Service. Names of students failing to register will be referred to the U.S. Department of Justice.

7. Sign a Statement of Educational Purpose. This form says that you intend to use GSL money only for expenses related to school.

8. Show financial need.

Of the eligibility requirements, the one that probably demands the most explanation is "financial need". Family income has a direct impact on whether you qualify for federal interest benefits. These interest benefits mean that the Department of Education will pay the total interest costs on your loan, as well as a "special allowance" interest to the lender to encourage lenders to participate in the GSL program. These payments continue as long as you remain in school (with some restrictions) or in grace or deferment. Most lenders will let you borrow only the amount eligible for federal interest benefits, since these are usually the only loan amounts that the lender can obtain the "guarantee" on.

The changes that became law in October 1986 removed the need verification for families whose income exceeded $30,000. Now all families, regardless of income, must demonstrate financial need in order to qualify for federal interest benefits and, thus, the GSL. What does this new requirement mean? It means that some families who had formerly qualified for GSLs may not be able to obtain loan aid for postsecondary education. The needs analysis is a complicated one, and individual circumstances vary. Due to the federal deficit and budget restriction, the government has imposed these new requirements in order to shift more of the burden of school costs to the student and family. Students may also have to rely on other programs. We'll describe some of these other programs in later chapters.

All applicants will have to undergo a "needs test". This calculation may be completed by one of the firms approved by Congress to calculate "expected family contribution" or by your high school counselor or college aid officer. Counselors and financial aid officers may utilize tables or computer programs to make these calculations. You may have already heard of the "Financial Aid Form" questionnaire which may be sent to the College Scholarship Service or the American College Testing Service for evaluation. (Addresses for these agencies are listed in Appendix B).

A "needs test" takes into consideration the family's income, assets, age and total annual expenses in several categories. This test determines the amount of college expense that can be borne by the parents or parent/guardian and by you, the student. The parent contribution and student contribution are combined to total the "Family Contribution" (FC). Need-based aid programs can provide funds only when the college budget exceeds the expected Family Contribution.

What does this needs test mean to your family? Your individual financial need could range from zero to several thousand dollars. Let's examine some individual families' finances and needs test data.

Our first sample family, Family A, has two children, one in college. The oldest parent is 46; the parents are married. The total family adjusted gross income is $33,000. The father is the only member employed, and is a personnel manager at a leading department store. This family had no payments to their IRA or KEOGH plan in 1986. Neither the parents nor the children had any untaxed income. (Untaxed income such as Veteran's Benefits must be disclosed separately).

Family A owns their home, which is valued at $55,000, and they have a mortgage balance of $29,000. Their child expects to have a summer job and earn $900. About $2,000 has been put in savings for him, and the student has saved $500 himself. They have no other business or investment assets. The family had medical expenses of only $750.

How does this family rate for financial aid? The needs test calculated that the parents could expect to contribute $2,486, and the student contribute $175 plus the student's expected summer savings of $700. The total "Family Contribution" or FC, then is $3,361.

The PELL Grant "Student Aid Index" (SAI) is 3,040 for this family. This means that they will be ineligible for a PELL Grant since the SAI must be below 1,500 in order to qualify. We will provide more PELL Grant information in Chapter 12— The PELL Grant.

This family will be expected to contribute a total of $3,361 toward this year's costs of postsecondary education for one child.

Need-based aid, such as the GSLP, will be afforded if the total cost of the education is over $3,361.

Family B also has four members and only one student applying for postsecondary education programs. The big difference is that now the oldest parent is 65 years old. Income is nearly the same at $29,000. Savings, medical expenses, summer employment, investments and business values are the same as with our first family. Now, however, the residence is valued at $55,000, but the mortgage balance is only $9,000.

The needs test, as the name implies, is designed to determine the expected financial needs the family may have in order to meet the costs of postsecondary education. Consideration will be given to the family's ability to meet these needs from their own resources. In Family B, we have changed the age of the parent dramatically and lowered the mortgage balance owed on their home.

The result of Family B's needs analysis is a family contribution of $3,236 and a PELL SAI of 3,850. Clearly the impact of the parent's age is offset by the increased equity in their home. An important concept of the needs test criteria is the family's ability to meet college costs by using their own income-producing abilities (income, age factor) as well as their assets (savings, home equity, net business or investment value).

Under the GSLP, student loans are available to undergraduate, graduate and professional students who meet all eligibility requirements. For students who currently have an outstanding loan at either a seven percent or nine percent interest rate, any additional amounts borrowed will be fixed at the same interest rate currently being charged. Since September 13, 1983, all new GSL borrowers are being charged an eight percent interest rate. Student borrowers are also subject to the five percent loan origination fee (see Chapter 1 — What is the GSLP?)

The table on page 23 shows the new borrowing limits for students entering programs after January 1, 1987:

Annual and aggregate lending limits are established by Congress. Like interest rates, these limits are also subject to legislative change. From 1976 to 1986 a student had been able to borrow up to $2,500 each year up to a total of $12,500 for undergraduate study. A graduate or professional student had a borrowing limit of $5,000 a year to a total of $25,000, including any undergraduate borrowing. The Higher Education Act was amended in 1986, and those amendments became law on October 17, 1986.

Lenders may have individual policies which will result in a loan amount less than the maximum allowed under the GSLP. For example, some financial institutions have a lower lending limit for freshman students who are first-time borrowers.

Type of Student	Annual Borrowing Limit	Total Amount Which May Be Borrowed
Freshman or Sophomore	$2,625	N/A
Junior or Senior	$4,000	$17,500
Graduate	$7,500	$54,750*
Professional	$7,500	$54,750*
*Includes any amounts borrowed as an undergraduate.		

Regardless of the GSLP or a lending institution's policies, a student may never borrow an amount more than the cost of the educational program, (minus any other financial assistance awarded. Examples of the latter are Veterans and Social Security educational benefits, work study, scholarships and grants.

If you receive a student loan, you will be responsible for repayment, including interest after school ends. For loans with an interest rate of nine percent and eight percent, repayment begins six months after the student borrower graduates or discontinues at least half-time study. On loans with an interest rate of seven percent, repayment begins nine to twelve months after graduation or discontinuation of at least half-time study.

Exact details of a repayment schedule must be worked out individually between the borrower and the lender. Furthermore, it's important to determine your student loan borrowing capacity (regardless of GSLP maximums!) by estimating your potential repayment capacity. Try to determine whether your estimated monthly salary, after taxes has been subtracted, will be adequate to meet living expenses as well as student loan repayment obligations and some discretionary spending (i.e. transportation, entertainment, etc.) Your school counselor, financial aid officer or lender may have materials or personal computer programs designed to estimate earnings and net incomes in various vocations and geographic areas of the country. Try to find out what you can expect to earn in the vocation you've chosen. Use this information to determine how much borrowing, if any, is realistically within your means. Don't borrow more than is possible to repay at a later date!

It's important that you realize, however, that such estimates are subject to limitations. For example, cost-of-living figures may be estimates for the entire United States. The location you choose can greatly affect earnings and expenses. Most financial experts feel that it is relatively safe to assume that salaries increase at about the same rate as living costs. What we're saying is that future jumps in inflation (which will obviously require more of your future earnings) will probably be offset by salary growth. The Bureau of Labor Statistics and Census both publish helpful statistics on regional costs and living expenses.

Application

Applying for a GSL is really very simple. Although several parties are involved, you, the borrower, may not have to personally interact with each. It's good to know, however, just for a better understanding of the federal aid program, who is involved.

Each of the parties we're about to describe must review, approve,and act on your application before a loan is issued. These participants in the GSLP process include lending institutions, academic institutions, state guarantee agencies (or their equivalent) and the federal government.

Lending institutions—Lenders are the people who actually lend you the money. Not every bank, savings & loan and credit union participate in the GSLP. In most communities, however, at least some of the lending institutions participate.

Where do you start looking for a lending institution?

Look into the bank where your family does business. If they don't participate in the GSLP, more than likely they can refer you to a lender that does. Many lenders will require that you live in their market area. Some may require you to have a checking account or other business relationship with them.

A participating lender is your best source of obtaining a GSL application. A financial aid officer or your school counselor may also be happy to provide the appropriate GSL forms. In some states, borrowers may also obtain applications directly from the State Guarantee Agency or the State Student Loan Agency or lender of last resort.

Academic Institutions—Once you complete the GSL application, submit this to the Financial Aid Office of the school you are attending, or to which you have been accepted for admission. Your school's Financial Aid Office is the first party to review a GSL application.

The responsibilities of the reviewer include: determining financial need, calculating the maximum loan allowable, validating information on the application, verifying academic standing, and supplying information on the cost of attendance. New regulations will require all Financial Aid Offices to "validate" the accuracy of income and needs information on nearly all GSL applicants. This means that you or your parents will have to supply some form of tax return or other income and expense information. Consult the Financial Aid Office for details of the types of information the particular school will be using. Once the Financial Aid Office assembles this information package, it is given to the lending institution of your choice.

Guarantee Agencies—After the academic institution has collected all pertinent information and a lending institution has agreed to provide the loan, the guarantee agency becomes involved. The guarantee agency verifies that a student has not been approved for a duplicate GSL during the current school year, that a student is not in default on a previous loan, that a student has not exceeded cumulative loan limits and that all supporting paperwork complies with federal requirements. But most important, the guarantee agency acts to approve the insurance on loan repayments to the lender. This act frees the lender to release funds to the student borrower.

Federal Government—Considering that a GSL is ultimately guaranteed by the federal government, naturally the latter plays an active role in program administration. Congress deals with legislative changes regarding interest rates, maximum loan amounts, financial need criteria, etc. The United States Department of Education is the rule-making and administrative authority in all GSL matters. Although the DOE is no longer directly involved in the issuance of guarantees, as they once were under the Federal Insured Student Loan (FISL), the DOE is indirectly involved with the financial stability of the respective guarantee agencies. Whether the agency is private- or state-funded, the Department of Education ensures that the operation is correctly administered, and that the loan collection activities are within acceptable limits. If the guarantor collects fewer defaulted loans than is acceptable the government, through its reinsurance, reimburses the agency on fewer and fewer loans. This helps keep the integrity of the program high and keeps the government's costs as low as possible.

The Department of Education also pays the lender the difference between the low rate of interest on a GSL (i.e. seven, eight or nine percent) and the higher interest rate the lender could earn on other more typical loans. The DOE also pays the face amount of interest on the loan as long as the borrower remains in school at least half-time and is making satisfactory progress.

As soon as you are accepted by a school, it's time to begin looking for a lender. So you won't feel overwhelmed when applying, we've briefly recapped what to expect.

1. Secure a GSL application from a lending institution, the Financial Aid Office of an academic institution, a guarantee agency or your counselor.

2. Fill out the student's section of the GSL application.

3. Submit the GSL application to the school's Financial Aid Office. Be sure to include all pertinent information and income or tax return data for the "verification" process.

4. The academic institution's Financial Aid Office completes its section, determining eligibility for interest benefits.

5. Take the application to the lender or request that the school mail the approved application to a lending institution for its approval.

6. If the lending institution approves the loan application, it will submit the loan to a guarantee agency.

7. The guarantee agency acts to either approve or reject the loan. NOTE: Many rejections occur because of incorrect or missing information. Be sure your birth date, Social Security number and school term data are all correct.

8. If the guarantee agency is able to insure the loan, the lender will contact you to obtain a signed note if they haven't already done so. This note is the legal document that describes the terms of the loan, such as the amount being borrowed, the interest rate in effect, and the repayment dates.

9. The lender will mail the check to you or to the school directly. The check may or may not be payable jointly. You may have access to the funds when registration is over, and you are enrolled.

Note: In many instances, schools have entered into agreements to forward applications directly to the guarantee agency. The school is "originating" the loans on behalf of the lender. This greatly speeds up the guarantee process. The process may be by mail, courier or electronic means.

Multiple Disbursement

Multiple disbursement means that the loan will be split into two increments or disbursements. Since most schools are on a semester or quarter basis, the timing of the second disbursement would be at or near the beginning of the second term of the academic year. When the school is on an hourly basis or other method, the second disbursement is usually a minimum of 90 days into the term. Previously, multiple disbursement was an option and was not required of all lenders.

This change limits the funds accessible to students. In other words, the funds to be used for the second semester or term won't be given out until they are to be used. This should not work any undue hardship on the student borrower. If the student is applying for loans to cover relatively small academic periods (i.e., a single semester or summer term) the multiple disbursement is not required.

As we've mentioned previously, the origination fee (five percent) and guarantee fees (up to three percent per year) are withheld from the loan proceeds before the check is written for you. If there are multiple disbursements, the total loan is divided into two or three allocations. The first of these will be smaller than in the following since, in addition to the origination fees, this first installment will usually deduct the guaranteed fee. Origination fees, but not guaranteed fees, are deducted from the remaining disbursements.

Repayment

Eventually a GSL must be repaid. Repayment and any possible exceptions to standard policy are discussed in more detail in Chapter 7—How Repayment Works. Once a GSL application is approved and funds are disbursed, then another phase of the process begins—repayment. In brief, a student borrower must begin repayment either after graduation or once enrollment status drops below the half-time level. Under normal policy, loan payments begin six months after you leave school. This interim period is called the "grace period".

During the grace period, it is recommended that you contact the lender in order to finalize repayment details. Current law dictates that a minimum monthly payment of $50 be made. Students with large outstanding loans may be expected to pay substantially more per month, so that the loan may be repaid within the allotted time limits. Repayment usually spans from a five- to 10-year period.

Responsibilities

As a GSL borrower, you have certain responsibilities. It's important that the loan be repaid according to the schedule provided by the lender. Notify the lender of anything that affects your repayment ability or eligibility for a deferment. (Chapter 7—How Repayment Works elaborates more on deferment policies.) Use the proceeds of a GSL only for tuition and other reasonable educational expenses. Always communicate with your lender. It is important that any change of student address or status becomes part of your lender's records. Inform your lender if, before the loan is repaid, you:

1. Graduate, withdraw or fall below half-time enrollment status.

2. Transfer to another school.

3. Fail to enroll for the period the loan was intended.

4. Change your name and/or address.

Chapter 4

The Parent (PLUS) Loan Program

The GSLP supports another program directed primarily to the parents of students attending participating schools. Under the guidelines of this program, a "parent" is defined as the natural or adoptive parent or the legal guardian. This program is called PLUS—an acronym for Parent Loans for Undergraduate Students.

PLUS has been in operation since 1981. Congress established this program to help parents borrow money for their children's postsecondary education. It allows parents to borrow up to $4,000 for each dependent undergraduate, graduate or professional student meeting eligibility requirements. For each dependent student, no more than $20,000 may be accumulated in unpaid loan principal.

To qualify for a PLUS loan, certain eligibility requirements must be met:

A parent borrowing under PLUS must:

1. Be the natural or adoptive parent of a dependent student or be the student's legal guardian.

2. Be a United States citizen or permanent resident.

3. Be free from default on a previous PLUS loan or any other type of student loan.

4. Be free from debt on a Pell, Basic or Supplemental Educational Opportunity Grant at the school being attended by the dependent student.

5. Have the lender's approval for the extension of credit.

The dependent student for whom the parent is borrowing must:

1. Be enrolled in a participating school on at least a half-time basis in an undergraduate, graduate or professional program.

2. Be a United States citizen or permanent resident.

3. Be free from default on any type of student loan and not owe a refund to any educational grant program (i.e., Pell, Basic Supplemental Educational Opportunity).

4. Be dependent, as determined by the academic institution, upon the parent for financial support.

5. Have utilized all eligibility for GSL funds.

Did you notice that nowhere in our eligibility listing did we list family income?

PLUS loans and family income are not directly related—you don't have to prove financial need in order to borrow money under the PLUS program. You may have already applied for and used regular student loan (GSL) funds, or have been denied aid based on the size of your "family contribution," (FC). The only way personal finances come into play directly with a PLUS loan is to prove that you have the financial capacity for loan repayment. This consideration is important since, unlike the GSLs, repayment begins within 60 days after disbursement of funds. Remember, PLUS loans may be used to meet part or all of your expected family contribution.

The annual interest rate on a PLUS loan is now a variable rate. This "variable" rate is a common means of setting consumer loan rates. A lender establishes a base or guide rate at the beginning of the loan, and as a predetermined index moves up or down, the consumer loan rate moves up or down. The new PLUS rate mechanism is tied to the 91-day Treasury Bill rate. Each December the Department of Education will set the rate for the coming year by adding 3.75 percent to the previous year's average 91-day Treasury Bill rate. The rates are capped at no higher than 12.0 percent. For 1987 the rate is 10.27 percent, APR. This rate structure is law for all loans, for school periods beginning after July 1. 1987. If you already had a PLUS loan, your lender should notify you and allow you the option of refinancing the loan with them or another lender in order to obtain the new lower, variable rate. Recently, the rate has been as high as 14 percent and as low as nine percent.

After the initial PLUS loan, you are encouraged to see the original lender if you need to borrow again. This may reduce the chance of having two or more $50 payments, when one payment may be lower. (Again, refer to Chapter 7—How Repayment Works for more information.)

The following chart shows sample payments at the 1986 12 percent fixed rate:

Principal	Years	Payment
$ 3,000	5	$ 66.72
9,000	8	97.50
12,000	10	172.20
15,000	10	215.25

These loans are made by financial institutions such as banks, savings and loans, credit unions, etc. Borrowers are able to obtain PLUS loans at generally more favorable rates and terms (up to 10 years to repay), without pledging personal assets. The DOE at times pays lenders an amount over and above the rate paid by the customer. The "special allowance" helps the lender obtain a yield closer to regular consumer credit. It also helps compensate for rate and dollar cost changes which may occur several times during the extended repayment period.

In this case, the lender does not retain an origination fee, as with the student GSL. They do, however, retain an insurance or guarantee fee. This fee is normally no more than three percent per year, for up to five years, based on the declining balance. The guarantee fee is a one-time charge which is forwarded to the guarantor (Higher Education Assistance Foundation, United Student Aid Fund or a state agency, for example,) in return for their guarantee of the loan. This guarantee works exactly like the one described for the GSL. It protects the lender against default or loss due to death, disability or bankruptcy.

In addition to proving the financial ability to support the loan, the lender will more than likely perform a credit check to ensure that the parent borrower has the demonstrated credit worthiness to obtain the loan. In fact , almost any time a lender makes a loan, a credit check is performed. A borrower's prior credit history is generally regarded as a good gauge of what to expect in the way of repayment. That's why it's so important to make payments on time. A bad credit history can result in the denial of future credit.

Application

Basically a PLUS borrower applies for the loan in the same way a student applies for a GSL. Unlike the latter, however, a PLUS borrower does not have to demonstrate financial need. You do have to show that there is an unfunded school cost which is over and above the amount expected to be received from other aid programs, such as the GSL. Only those amounts up to but not exceeding the cost of attendance are eligible for funding with a PLUS loan.

Let's briefly recap the steps you typically go through when applying for a PLUS loan:

1. Obtain an application from an academic institution, lending institution or guarantee agency.

2. The parent must complete and sign the first section of the application.

3. The student must complete and sign the student section of the application.

4. Send the application to the school's Financial Aid Office. The latter must then complete the appropriate section.

5. The borrower submits the application to the lending institution.

6. The lending institution may ask that a consumer loan or credit application be completed. This can usually be accomplished in person, by phone or by mail.

7. Once credit approval has been given, the lending institution forwards the application to a guarantee agency.

8. After the loan is secured by a guarantee agency, the lender will require you to sign the disclosures and a Promissory Note. This note specifies the amount being borrowed, applicable interest rates and repayment terms, along with other responsibilities. By signing the note, the borrower assumes responsibility for paying back the loan.

9. Loan proceeds are then disbursed by the lending institution. The lender may either send the disbursement check directly to the school, the borrower and/or the student.

While describing the steps you normally go through when applying for a PLUS loan, we didn't elaborate on the roles played by the parties involved. Each plays basically the same role as that described in Chapter 3—The Student Loan.

In many ways student and PLUS loans are alike. Both loans must be used only for education purposes. Congress controls policies like interest rates and repayment terms, and during the application process, the same parties are involved.

The basic difference between a student and PLUS loan is the intent behind each. Congress established PLUS loans as a way to help families who want to assume financial responsibility for their children's postsecondary education. In the case of a student loan, this responsibility is assumed by the student-borrower rather than the parent., However, for a PLUS loan the parent has full responsibility for repayment; it is a credit transaction on the parent's part, rather than the student's.

The PLUS program has, however, experienced only limited growth. Part of this can be attributed to a general lack of awareness many have about this form of student financial aid. The PLUS loans are one of the least publicized student aid programs. As a result of the 1986 amendments to the Higher Education Act, the PLUS loan program is expected to take on new significance in the financing of postsecondary education.

Other Alternatives for Parent Borrowers

There are other alternatives to the PLUS program. We often hear more about these, though none are strictly education programs. If the parent borrows to assume some or all financial responsibility for the student's education, you may wish to explore some of these ideas.

The 1986 Congressional session brought another significant legislative change, the Tax Law revisions. Deductions are severely curtailed or eliminated. See your tax preparer or advisor for detailed information on the allowable interest deductions.

Many parent borrowers may borrow against cash values from whole-life insurance policies. The rates and repayment terms are usually very favorable. Rates as low as five to six percent may be had, and payments may be limited to the accrued finance charge without initially reducing the principal. If you own equity in your home, you may wish to consider a home equity loan. These loans (really mortgages) also are structured to offer extended repayment terms at usually very favorable rates when compared to other consumer loans. Approximately one half of all home equity loans are made to parents borrowing to finance their children's educational goals.

Don't forget those series E or EE U.S. Savings Bonds purchased through payroll deduction plans. Since U.S. Savings Bonds currently average 10 years to reach maturity, many parents who choose this method of financing their child's education begin purchasing bonds before the child even starts elementary school. Funds may also be available when needed by making long-term periodic investments in your employer's thrift or company savings plan. This alternative, too, should be carefully evaluated with a competent tax representative in order to evaluate the impact of the 1986 tax law changes.

What's the best solution if parents want to finance their child's education? That depends on personal circumstances. For some people, the PLUS programs is the best idea, particularly if they do not have whole-life insurance policies or enough equity in their home. Starting a savings plan when children are young is not always feasible—personal incomes may be too low then.

Our best advice is to take your time and explore all alternatives. Also, do it early enough in the child's life in order to adequately plan ahead. Preparing for a college education isn't something that can be done overnight. A financial plan, prepared carefully and reviewed periodically, will help you make these decisions with the right information. (See Chapters 17 and 18 on "Financial Planning" for useful guidelines.)

In the previous chapters we introduced the concept of need-based financial aid programs. Our first two samples, Family A and Family B, each had expected family contributions of over $3,000. The PLUS loan program with its annual limit of $4,000 is more than enough to meet the family contributions of these sample families.

The Supplemental Loan Program (Formerly ALAS)

In Chapter 4—The Parent (PLUS) Loan Program, we introduced the idea of the PLUS program. Our main emphasis was on parents and how this program enables them to meet the financial obligations associated with a child's education. Now we'll look at another financial option offered by the GSLP.

The PLUS program has another aspect—the Supplemental Loan Program, formerly the Auxiliary Loan to Assist Students (ALAS) program. This program may also be known as the Jeffords Loan Program, for Congressman Jeffords, its sponsor. Before exploring the details associated with this particular type of financing, let's define exactly what is meant by the term "independent". In order to be considered an independent, self-supporting individual under federal criteria, specific circumstances must be met. An independent student CANNOT:

1. Be claimed as an exemption for federal income tax purposes by parents or guardians.

2. Receive less than $4,000 of income and benefits per year.

In addition, you will be considered independent if you:

3. Are over age 22.

4. Are a military veteran.

5. Are an orphan or ward of the court.

6. Have legal dependents other than a spouse.

If you fail to meet any of the above provisions, the federal government regards you as a "dependent student". There is but one exception. Married students must prove only independence for the year financial assistance is requested, not for the preceding year also.

When filling out an application for a supplemental loan as an independent student, you will be asked question similar to the eligibility criteria we listed. Once satisfied that you do fit into the independent student category, other eligibility issues must also be resolved.

Students requesting a supplemental loan on their own behalf must:

1. If an undergraduate student, be independent of financial support from their family according to federal regulations. See the dependency determinations listed earlier for the "independent student".

2. Or, be a graduate or professional student.

3. Be enrolled or accepted for admission at an eligible school on at least a half-time basis.

4. Be making satisfactory progress as determined by the academic institution.

5. Be either a United States citizen or a permanent resident with proper visa.

6. Not be in default on any type of student loan or PLUS loans.

7. Not owe a refund on any educational grant program (i.e. Pell, SEOG).

8. Not have exceeded the maximum allowable loan amounts of the PLUS program.

9. Be capable of repaying the loan. The lending institution will make this determination.

If you are an independent student and meet other eligibility requirements, the supplemental loan program currently offers loans at the new variable interest rate. As previously mentioned, Congress authorizes the loan amounts and interest rates applicable under the PLUS/SUPPLEMENTAL/GSL programs. These amounts and rates are subject to change.

For example, during your freshman and sophomore years you borrowed $2,500 each as a student borrower under the GSLP for a total of $5,000. In your junior year, you get married and become an independent student. You may also now borrow under the PLUS/SUPPLEMENTAL program. You may borrow a total of $4,000 per academic period, excluding any current GSL borrowing. The aggregate limits for undergraduate independent students is $20,000. This is in addition to regular GSL loans, which could total $17,500.

AGGREGATE BORROWING LIMITS		
Type of Student	Annual Borrowing Limit	Total Amount Which May Be Borrowed
Undergraduate*	$4,000**	$20,000
Graduate	$4,000	$20,000
Professional	$4,000	$20,000
*Undergraduate means independent undergraduate		
**Includes amounts borrowed under GSL for same period		

The needs test for an independent student varies from that of the dependent student's family contribution calculation. Suppose that you are an independent student who has no dependents. In this case, the Carter family, suppose your annual gross income was $12,000 and you paid $900 in federal tax, were under the age of 26 and had assets of $3,000. Your expected family contribution could be as high as $3,400. If, as in the case of the Dixon family, you had dependents, the family contribution calculations then more closely approximate the steps utilized for dependent students. With the addition of dependents, a deduction from your income is taken for reasonable living expenses, an employment expense, a medical dental expense allowance and an educational expense allowance. In the example of the Dixon family, with one dependent child and the same income as the Carter family, the expected family contribution would fall to $0. Chapter 6—The Needs Test will provide additional explanations.

Payment

An an independent student borrowing under the PLUS/SUPPLEMENTAL program, you will be subject to deferred or immediate payment options. A full-time student borrower may have the principal payments deferred. Interest charges must be paid periodically or capitalized (added) to the borrowed amounts and repaid one you leave school. The guarantee agencies generally prefer that students on full-time deferments assume responsibility for paying the interest charges as they accrue. The lender can arrange to bill the student monthly or quarterly. We'll have more on deferment and repayment policies in Chapter 7--How Repayment Works.

Borrowers not eligible for full-time deferments or borrowers who opt for immediate repayment must begin interest and principal payments within 60 days of disbursement. Payments are a minimum of $50 per month and can extend over a maximum period of 60 months. Repayment must be completed within 120 months of disbursement.

Although the PLUS/SUPPLEMENTAL loan is guaranteed to the lender, the lenders must satisfy themselves that the borrower is able to repay the loan and that he or she has a satisfactory credit history. These loans do not involve a collateral requirement, and collateral cannot be substituted for ability to pay or good credit.

When determining ability to pay, the borrower who is going into immediate repayment must demonstrate that his/her current monthly budget can support a loan payment. After fixed payments (rent, utilities, auto and other loan payments) are deducted from income, the borrower must have enough funds to meet the remaining living expenses (food, entertainment, insurance, medical) with enough left over still to make the proposed loan payment.

Lenders follow many different guidelines in analyzing the monthly budget. One rule of thumb is that the fixed, regular expenses, including this loan payment, not exceed 50 percent of the monthly take-home pay. You should review your own finances carefully and fully discuss your capabilities with the lender before entering into the loan agreement.

Full-time independent undergraduate borrowers may defer the principal and interest until falling below half-time attendance or making less than satisfactory progress. In these instances, the lender will want to know if future earnings can support the loan repayment, along with other living expenses. Obviously, these considerations must include the overall economic conditions in your area, as well as the marketability of your field of study in the local labor market.

Deferment

The term "deferment" means that the borrower meets specified conditions which allow postponement of principal and/or interest payments. While a loan is in deferment status, the federal government continues to subsidize the loan by making any special allowance payments.

Deferments under the PLUS/SUPPLEMENTAL program differ slightly than those for regular GSL borrowers. The PLUS/SUPPLEMENTAL borrower is still responsible for interest payments during any approved period of deferment. Chapter 7—How Repayment Works contains a complete discussion of deferment.

Chapter 6

The Needs Test

One of the significant changes to come as the result of the 1986 amendments to the Higher Education Act was the requirement that all applicants, regardless of income, must now prove need. The Guaranteed Student Loan program, whether it is for an undergraduate student, graduate student, parent or independent student is a "need-based" program. What is meant by "need based?" Let's compare the GSL for the moment with the Pell Grant program. You'll learn more about the Pell Grant in Chapter 12—The Pell Grant

The Pell Grant is an entitlement program. This means that if the applicant meets certain minimum requirements, then there is an award through the Pell Grant system. Congress funds the Pell for all those applicants who are "entitled". The GSL, on the other hand, is a program that supports only a fixed number of loans. When or if the total number of applicants exceeds funding, the loans could be cut off. All applicants beginning school on or after January 1, 1987 must complete some form of needs analysis.

The needs test calculations are designed to provide the applicant with the amount of parent and student contributions to the total cost of education. This contribution is the amount that the family is expected to pay toward the student's college budget.

What is meant by the "Family Contribution"? What can be done to estimate or calculate the amount of need that the student's family may have? These questions are important, and are some of the ones most commonly asked at this time. Before we review the usual questions asked about the needs analysis, let's examine the data elements used during the needs analysis.

Section 474 of Public Law 99-498, the Higher Education Amendments of 1986, lists the following data elements to be considered in the needs analysis. They are:

1. The available income of (A) the student and his or her spouse, or (B) the student (and spouse) and the student's parents, in the case of a dependent student;

2. The number of dependents in the family of the student;

3. The number of dependents in the family of the student who are enrolled in, on at least half-time basis, a program of postsecondary education and for whom the family may reasonably be expected to contribute to their postsecondary education;

4. The net assets of (A) the student and his or her spouse, and (B) the student (and spouse) and the student's parents, in the case of a dependent student;

5. The marital status of the student;

6. Any unusual medical and dental expenses of (A) the student and the student's parents, in the case of a dependent student, or (B) the student and his or her dependents, in the case of an independent student;

7. The number of dependent children other than the student enrolled in a private elementary or secondary institution and the unreimbursed tuition paid (A) in the case of a dependent student, by the student's parents for such dependent children, or (B) in the case of an independent student with dependents, by the student or his or her spouse for such dependent children who are so enrolled;

8. The additional expenses incurred (A) in the case of a dependent student, when both parents of the student are employed or when the family is headed by a single parent who is employed or (B) in the case of an independent student, when both the student and his or her spouse are employed or when the employed student qualifies as a surviving spouse or as a head of a household under Section 2 of the Internal Revenue Code of 1954.

Remember, this is the list of data elements *which are considered*, not the manner in which they are considered. We will review some additional case studies to show how changes in these elements may change the amount of the Family Contribution. There are alternative sources for obtaining actual or estimated family contribution calculations. These are listed later in this chapter, and their complete addresses are provided in Appendix B.

The first needs test was the result of the Omnibus Reconciliation Act of 1981. One of the key points of this legislation was the issue of family contributions. Congress believed that families in higher income brackets could afford to meet all or at least some of their children's education expenses, thus reducing the interest subsidies paid by the federal government on GSL's. This was the topic of debate again in Congress in 1986. Now, however, Congress believes that more and more families should shoulder the burden of their children's postsecondary education expenses.

A standard formula which considers those data elements above is used to determine how much a family is expected to contribute towards a child's education. The formula calculates the Expected Family Contribution (EFC), or Family Contribution (FC). This is the amount expected to be paid by the family before any aid is applied towards the school budget. Remember that many of these items are variable from family to family and year to year.

Just because your friend or neighbor qualified does not mean that your qualification is automatic. It is important to do a needs analysis each year of college or other postgraduate school. You may find that the family contribution is lower than you'd have imagined.

The following case studies will show how different family circumstances influence the final calculation of family contribution. It is important to note that Congress intends to encourage each family to pay as much of the postsecondary expense as their own income and asset situation allows. The methodology considers the age of the oldest parent and allows the older parents to protect more of their assets (see Table 3). Parents with a relatively comfortable income are expected to be able to support a significant amount of the school costs. Even if your family does not have the cash on hand to "just write a check" for the total school cost, they may be expected to borrow or convert some of their assets to cash in order to meet their portion of the total school budget.

Family E is a family of three members; a single parent with one child seeking financial aid. The Adjusted Gross Income (AGI) is $25,000, federal tax $3,000; the student projects an income of $900 this summer. The student has cash and savings of $500, and the parent has $2,000. The home is valued at $25,000 with a mortgage of $21,000. There are no other investments. This family has a total family contribution of $2,448.

Family F is a family of five with both parents married. The family income is $41,000, federal tax $5,600. There are no unusual medical expenses, and the student expects an income this summer of $900. The student has savings of $500; the parents, $3,000. The home is worth $55,000 and has a mortgage of $30,000. There are no other investments or assets.

This family's expected contribution is $4,228. Why did the contribution change? We will examine the individual components of the uniform methodology in these two cases to determine why they were different.

The income computations for a parent are, in general, the total income minus:

    A. Federal income taxes,
    B. An allowance for state and other taxes (See Table 1),
    C. An allowance for Social Security taxes,
    D. A standard maintenance allowance (See Table 2),
    E. An employment expense allowance, and
    F. A medical-dental expense allowance.

This example will take you step-by-step through the calculations for the Family E:

Step One

Gross Income	$ 25,000
Federal Tax	– 3,000
State Tax	– 1,500
Social Sec. (7.15%)	– 1,573
Standard Maint.	–10,440
Employment Exp.	– 2,100
Medical/Dental	– 0
Educational Exp.	– 0
Available Income	$ 6,387

Step Two

Parents Income Supplemental from Assets

Net Worth	$ 6,000
Minus Asset Protection Allowance Table 3)	-38,300
Asset Conversion Rate (Table 4)	
Assets ($6,000) × .028 =	
Assets Assessed	168.00
Assessment of income (Table 5)	1,405.14
Parent Contribution	1,573.14

Step Three

Add the Student Contribution	175.00
Add the Student Summer Savings	700.00
Total Family Contribution	2,448.14

We will compare the calculations for Family F:

Step One

Income	$ 41,000.00
Federal Tax	- 5,600.00
State Tax	- 2,606.00
Social Security	- 2,931.00
Standard Maintenance	-15,210.00
Employment Exp.	- 2,100.00
Medical/Dental	- 0
Educational	- 0
Available Income	$ 12,553.00

Step Two

Parents Income Supplemental from Assets

Net Worth	28,000.00
Minus Asset Protection Allowance (Table 3)	-33,300.00
Asset Conversion Rate (Table 4)	
Net Worth (28,000) × .009 =	
Assessment	252.00
Income Assessment (Table 5)	3,101.00
Parent Contribution	3,353.00

Step Three

Add the student contribution	$ 175.00
Add the student summer savings	700.00
Total Family Contribution	$4,228.00

It is important to note that we did not itemize the student contribution. The student contribution is relatively simple. First, there is a mandatory self-help amount of $700 for first-year undergraduate students and $900 for any other students, (or 70 percent of their total income, whichever is greater.)

Student assets are assessed by a flat rate of 35 percent. This assessment is far greater than that found in the two examples above. We encourage you to seek competent financial advice on the management of assets which your student may accumulate. This may enable you to reduce those assessed at the flat 35 percent rate.

The tables included in this chapter are for estimates only. They provide computation tools for the dependent student's parent contribution. The methodology for independent students with and without dependents can be found as part of Public Law 99-498, Sections 477 and 478.

Although these computations and examples may seem arbitrary, we want you to realize that we could not include examples, depicting all possible situations. One important aspect of this law and the authority given to the Financial Aid Administrator is the ability to act in the best interest of the student applicant. What this means is that the financial aid administrators are given fairly wide discretion to make necessary adjustments to the family contribution computations. These adjustments must be supported by adequate documentation and are to be made only for the treatment of individual students with special circumstances.

The methodology presented here is only one of several means to determine your family's expected Family Contribution. Check with your high school counselor. He or she may have tables and formulas which can be used to approximate the expected Family Contribution. Many schools are equipped with computer programs which, when correctly supplied with family asset and income figures, will yield a close approximation of the expected Family Contribution. Your respective state agency may conduct a needs test through its own GSL or Pell Grant process. Various state agencies use their own application forms.

Many states and most colleges depend on the financial aid form application and evaluation done by the College Scholarship Service or the American College Testing Program. (See Appendix B, List of State Agencies, for a description of their services and addresses.) These services will analyze the data supplied on the application form and provide your family's Expected Family Contribution to several colleges at your direction. The fees for this service are reasonable, and it is a reliable method of obtaining an accurate FC calculation. These firms have been approved by the Department of Education to use the same method to determine family contributions.

The Expected Family Contribution is static—in other words, it stays the same—no matter where you plan to attend school. Overall school costs will have an effect on the amount of aid you may be eligible to receive. For example, if your family contribution were $3,000, and you attend a school whose total educational budget is $4,500, you would be eligible for $1,500 of aid to meet the difference. If you attend a school with a total budget of $2,900 you would be ineligible for aid. Your family contribution already exceeds the amount of your educational costs.

The education costs remaining after the family contribution are the costs that can be met by the various programs we've discussed. The chart below summarizes those programs and the applicable borrowers:

Borrower	Program
Dependent Student	Guaranteed Student Loan
Independent Student	Supplemental Loan (Formerly ALAS)
Parent of Dependent	Parent Loan (PLUS)**

**The PLUS Loan can be used to meet the family contribution! See Chapter 4—The Parent (PLUS) Loan Program.

The tables that follow are for estimating purposes only to enable parents and students to focus more clearly on their own situation.

TABLE 1

The allowance for state and other taxes is equal to an amount determined by multiplying total income by a percentage determined according to the following table:

| | Parents' Total Income | |
| | Less Than $15,000 | $15,000 or More |
Parents' Residence	The percentage is:	
Alaska, Puerto Rico, Wyoming	3	2
American Samoa, Guam, Louisiana, Nevada, Texas Trust Territory, Virgin Islands	4	3
Florida, South Dakota, Tennessee, New Mexico	5	4
North Dakota, Washington	6	5
Alabama, Arizona, Arkansas, Indiana, Mississippi, Missouri, Montana, New Hampshire, Oklahoma, West Virginia	7	6
Colorado, Connecticut, Georgia, Illinois, Kansas, Kentucky	8	7
California, Delaware, Idaho, Iowa, Nebraska, North Carolina, Ohio, Pennsylvania, South Carolina, Utah, Vermont, Virginia, Canada, Mexico	9	8
Maine, New Jersey	10	9
District of Columbia, Hawaii, Maryland, Massachusetts, Oregon, Rhode Island	11	10
Michigan, Minnesota	12	11
Wisconsin	13	12
New York	14	13

TABLE 2. Standard Maintenance Allowance

The standard maintenance allowance is the amount of reasonable living expenses that would be associated with maintenance of an individual or family.

| Family Size | Number in College | | | | | For Each Addit'l Subtract |
	1	2	3	4	5	
2	$ 8,380	$ 6,950				
3	10,440	9,010	$ 7,580			
4	12,890	11,460	10,030	$ 8,600		
5	15,210	13,780	12,350	10,920	$ 8,490	
6	17,790	16,360	14,930	13,500	12,070	$ 1,430
Each add'l.	2,010	2,010	2,010	2,010	2,010	

TABLE 3. Asset Protection Allowance

"Asset Protection Allowance" is calculated according to the following:

Age of Oldest Parent	And There Are	
	Two Parents	One Parent
	Then the asset protection allowance is	
25 or less	0	0
26	1,900	1,500
27	3,900	3,000
28	5,800	4,500
29	7,800	6,100
30	9,700	7,600
31	11,700	9,100
32	13,600	10,600
33	15,600	12,100
34	17,500	13,600
35	19,500	15,100
36	21,400	16,600
37	23,400	18,200
38	25,300	19,700
39	27,300	21,200
40	29,200	22,700
41	30,000	23,200
42	30,800	23,800
43	31,600	24,200
44	32,500	24,800
45	33,300	25,400
46	34,200	26,100
47	35,200	26,700
48	36,100	27,200
49	37,300	27,900
50	38,300	28,800
51	39,600	29,500
52	40,900	30,300
53	42,000	31,000
54	43,400	32,000
55	44,800	32,800
56	46,300	33,800
57	48,100	34,600
58	49,700	35,700
59	51,600	36,800
60	53,300	37,900
61	55,300	39,000
62	57,400	40,200
63	59,600	41,400
64	61,800	42,600
65 or more	64,100	44,100

TABLE 4. Asset Conversion Rate
The asset conversion rate is determined as follows:

A. If the parental net worth minus the asset protection allowance is equal to or greater than zero, the conversion rate is 12%;

B. If such parental net worth minus such asset protection allowance is less than zero, and the parents' contribution from available income is greater than $15,000, the conversion rate is zero;

C. If such parental net worth minus such asset protection allowance is less than zero, and the available income is equal to or greater than zero but less than $15,000, the conversion rate (rounded to 3 decimal places) is equal to 6% multiplied by a fraction —

   1. The numerator of which is equal to $15,000 minus such parents' available income; and

   2. The denominator of which is $15,00; and

D. If such parental net worth minus such asset protection allowance is less than zero and the available income is equal ot or less than zero, the conversion rate is 6%.

TABLE 5. Assessment Schedule
The Adjusted Available Income (AAI) is assessed according to the following:

Parents' Assessment from Adjusted Available Income (AAI)

If AAI is —	Then the Assessment is —
Less than $3,409	–$750
$3,409 to $7,500	22% of AAI
$7,501 to $9,400	$1,650 + 25% of AAI over $7,500
$9,401 to $11,300	$2,125 + 29% of AAI over $9,400
$11,301 to $13,200	$2,676 + 34% of AAI over $11,300
$13,201 to $15,100	$3,322 + 40% of AAI over $13,200
$15,501 or more	$4,082 + 47% of AAI over $15,100

Chapter 7

How Repayment Works

The term "repayment" refers to the act of paying back a loan. It is usually done in monthly installments, and the amount paid is normally divided between the principal and interest owed.

If you are a parent borrowing under the PLUS program, repayment begins almost immediately after funds are disbursed. The first payment is due within 60 days after the loan is made. For parent borrowers, repayment of a PLUS loan generally ranges from three to ten years, ten years being the maximum repayment period allowed. If a PLUS borrower dies or becomes totally and permanently disabled, the United States Department of Education cancels the debt by paying the lender the total amount owed. Note, however, that PLUS loans jointly obtained by two parents or by two legal guardians will not be eligible for disability or death claim payment unless both borrowers are disabled or deceased.

An independent student borrowing under the PLUS/Supplemental program is obligated to begin interest payments within only 60 days after disbursement. Repayment of principal may be deferred until the independent student withdraws, graduates or falls below half-time status. Deferments may also be granted once the borrower is no longer in school. The same conditions outlined later in this chapter for GSLP student borrowers also apply to independent students asking for deferment of payments.

Students borrowing under the GSLP must contact their lenders as soon as they leave school in order to establish a repayment schedule. The amount of each payment depends upon the size of the debt, but the minimum monthly payment is now $50. Of course the more you borrow, the higher the payment. Beginning on January 1, 1987, lenders are required to provide the student with a chart and worksheet that can be used to project future payment, based on the present level of borrowing. We've included a worksheet in Appendix C for your use. This way at least you won't risk an unaffordable surprise right after graduation. Never, and we repeat never, borrow more than you feel comfortable repaying.

Each loan obtained under the GSL program will be consolidated automatically, provided it is obtained from the same lender. It is important that you try to continue to borrow from the same lender, year after year, for several reasons. A consolidated payment may be less than several $50 minimum payments to different lenders. Furthermore, the lender becomes familiar with you. Another revision made in the 1986 amendments permits lenders to consolidate loans held by different lenders. As of this writing the procedures have not been published. If you now have outstanding student loans, particularly with more than one lender, please check with your lender or guarantor if you are interested in consolidating your loan balances. This can save both of you time when applying for additional funds.

If you change schools or programs, communicate changes to your lender. Keeping the lender informed will enhance your chance of obtaining future loans.

At times, lenders withdraw from the GSL program. If this happens with your lender, you should consider two things if you plan on borrowing again for school:

1. Ask for the recommendation of a lender who can continue to service your GSL needs. Don't just think of GSLs. If the lender is no longer making GSLs, he will likely quit making PLUS/SUPPLEMENTAL loans too.

2. Determine if your lender has or will sell your outstanding loans to a participating lender or servicer. Loans purchased by another lender may be consolidated. Consolidation means that you, the borrower, won't have loans from more than one lender. Remember, loan payments are a minimum of $50. Each loan you have with a different lender will require a separate $50 minimum payment unless they can be consolidated.

Repayment for a GSLP student borrower begins six months after withdrawal or graduation from school or if you drop below half-time status. (Nine to twelve months if the loan rate is seven percent). The period of time between leaving school and beginning repayment is called the "grace period". Your Promissory Note will clearly state the length of the grace period applicable to the loan being made.

Five years is a fairly common repayment term for a student borrower. The lender may allow no more than 10 years. You do have the right, however, to repay the entire loan or any portion of it at any time.

If you borrow for school periods beginning after July 1, 1988, your repayment interest rates will be on a two-tier system. For the first four years of repayment, the rate will be the statutory eight percent. But beginning with the fifth year of repayment, the rate will jump to 10 percent. This is because the program's costs are being shifted to the borrower. Remember we have discussed the "special allowance" that the Department of Education pays to the lenders. The 10 percent rate, in effect, removes the special allowance from those loan periods. In addition when the 91-day Treasury Bill rate plus 3.25 percent (special allowance rate) is less than 10 percent, the difference you are paying will be credited to the principal balance of the loan. What we're saying is that you will never have to bear an effective cost of over T-bill rate plus 3.25 percent. The lender will always receive no more than T-Bill plus 3.25 percent, either from the Department of Education or the borrower, but of course not both.

The United States Department of Education pays the lender all interest due on a student-borrowed loan as long as the student remains in school on at least a half-time basis and is making satisfactory progress. There is no obligation for the student to finance subsequent years schooling through the GSLP. Federal interest payments continue during the grace period and any deferment periods.

Death or Disability Claims

The lending institution may file a claim for payment within 60 days of death or notification. Disability claims must be certified by a physician. Remember our describing the "insurance" fee deducted from the loan proceeds? This insurance is for both death or disability claims as well as instances of default.

Instances of default arise when the borrower is unwilling or unable to make payments on the debt. Lenders recognize that at times borrowers can come under severe financial hardship. Any time your income is interrupted, you should see your lender. There are statutory provisions that just may provide the relief you need. Congress saw fit to include many safeguards for the student borrower. We'll cover them in later sections of this chapter.

In the event that you file a personal bankruptcy, the lender will submit a claim to the guarantor for the outstanding balance of all GSL debts. After the claims process, you, the borrower, will then be expected to make loan payments to the guarantor. Guaranteed Student Loans are NOT dischargeable under the Bankruptcy Code.

Forbearance

Any time that the lender allows payments to be reduced, stopped temporarily or grants an extension of time, the lender is granting "forbearance". Lenders are encouraged to grant forbearances in instances that require extraordinary aid to the student borrower. In many instances, forbearance is granted in cases that did not qualify for a deferment. A lender does not have to grant a forbearance. Such a decision is solely at the discretion of the lending institution.

Deferments

Both GSLP student borrowers and SUPPLEMENTAL independent borrowers are eligible for deferments. A deferment delays the repayment schedule. A delinquent borrower may be granted a deferment, but only if he or she is eligible. A borrower in default may not be granted a deferment even if such borrower meets eligibility requirements.

Deferments can be granted for several specific instances. Below is a listing of the time limits for the various deferment categories and the eligibility requirements. (These time limits are in addition to the regular grace periods.)

A. No-Time Limitation

1. Pursuing studies on a full-time basis at a school participating in the GSLP. In order to officially grant a deferment, the borrower who does not leave his/her

grace period or in-school status, need merely attend half-time and make satisfactory progress in order to delay repayment. All eligibility requirements for the GSLP, such as being a United States citizen or national must be met.

2. Receiving rehabilitation training under an approved program or scheduled to begin receiving such training within three months.

3. Participating full-time in an eligible graduate fellowship program.

B. Three-Year Limitation

1. Serving active duty in the United States armed forces or serving as an officer in the Commissioned Corps of the Public Health Service.

2. Serving as a full-time volunteer in a tax-exempt organization, which is comparable to volunteer service in the Peace Corps; full-time volunteer service in the Peace Corps; or full-time volunteer service in a program administered by ACTION.

3. Temporarily totally disabled (or is unable to work because of the care required for a dependent who is temporarily totally disabled).

4. Teachers who are teaching in certain geographic areas where there are teacher shortages or in subject areas where there are teacher shortages. The shortages will be defined by the Secretary, DOE in conjunction with the chief school officer of the state or appropriate private official. You should check with the local school jurisdiction to determine if you qualify.

5. Serving as an active duty member of the National Oceanic and Atmospheric Administration Corps.

C. Two-Year Limitation

1. Serving in an internship or residency program approved by the United States Secretary of Education. Such a program is one that must be successfully completed in

order to receive recognition required to begin professional practice or service.

D. One-Year Limitation

1. Conscientiously seeking but unable to find full-time employment in the United States. Full-time employment is defined as employment which the borrower is physically able to perform, for at least 30 hours per week, and is expected to last at least six months. Unemployment deferments may be granted for no longer than six months on a single request. A second consecutive request for up to six months may be granted, but that is the maximum allowed. Unemployment deferments are a one-time benefit.

2. A working mother entering or reentering the workforce and earning less than $1 above the federal minimum wage.

E. Special Six-Month Parental Deferment.

This is for the mother or father of a newborn child. Details were unavailable at press time. Please consult with your lender or guarantor for details.

Can a Loan Be Canceled?

Student loans may be canceled as a result of death or disability claim payment. The Department of Defense sponsors a program which will repay portions of the student loan for active service in the Army, Navy, Air Force, Marines, as well as the National Guard and Reserve units. The debt that is canceled is based on the length of enlistment. This is a popular enlistment incentive.

What if You Fail To Repay a Loan?

If you fail to repay a student loan, you may be subject to collection activities by the lender, the guarantor, and the Department of Education. These collection activities may include legal steps such as civil suits and attachment of wages or property. Attempts are being made to attach tax refunds of federal workers who've defaulted on student loans.

Recent legislation requires that all disbursements of student loans be reported to local credit bureaus. This means that a record of your repayment on any GSL will be maintained from the day the loan was originally made. These same credit records are checked by a lender when they are considering making an auto or personal loan, a home loan, or issuing a credit card.

Summary

Loan repayment may be one of the most complex and misunderstood aspects of the GSL program. So we can make sure that you remember the major points, we've provided you with an easy-to-understand list of the important ones:

1. Repayment begins after the end of the "grace period".

2. Be sure to communicate with your lender during the grace period to ensure that the repayment terms fit your financial situation.

3. Be especially careful not to borrow from more than one lender if possible. Each loan may require a minimum of $50 monthly payment.

4. Consecutive loans throughout your schooling may be consolidated into one payment by your lender/servicer.

5. Deferments are available for a variety of situations.

6. Deferments are applicable ONLY if you have entered into repayment.

7. Defaulted loans will become a part of your credit file and can, therefore, result in the denial of future borrowings.

Chapter 8

The Economics of Credit

Why is a lending institution willing to make loans when repayment may be delayed several years?

One feature of the government program that lenders find attractive is the "in-school interest subsidy". Through interest subsidies to lenders, the federal government pays the interest due on loans made to student borrowers until the repayment period begins. These interest subsidies continue throughout the grace period and any subsequent deferment periods.

By subsidizing student loans, the federal government removes from student borrowers the burden of making any type of loan payments as long as they are attending school on at least a half-time basis. Furthermore, the lender is assured of receiving timely interest payments on loan balances outstanding. Until the repayment period begins, the only costs to the student borrower are "origination fees" and insurance premiums.

The Omnibus Budget Reconciliation Act of 1981 created a five percent loan origination fee on GSLs to help offset the lender's costs of making these loans. When the loan is made, significant clerical and operation costs are incurred by the lender. Interest is paid quarterly by the Department of Education, so a loan made early in the quarter will not yield interest to the lending institution for 90 days or more. The origination fee helps defray these costs. This fee also reduces the total amount of interest the government is obligated to pay on the loan. Since it is deducted from the loan check and from the next quarterly interest due billing, the lender and the Department of Education are both compensated.

The Graham Rudman Budget Reconciliation Act of 1986 imposed a temporary 5.5 percent origination fee. The current fee is once again five percent. There is the possibility that, for the next several years, the origination fee could be increased because of budget deficits.

Another way the federal government attracts lenders to participate in the GSLP is through the payment of "special allowances".

Rarely is today's interest market stable for long. Your lender may be making loans at nine percent one year and the next at fifteen percent. Because of the fast-moving changes in interest markets, many lenders are writing an increasing number of variable rate loans. Your family's most recent auto or home loan was very likely calculated on a variable or adjustable rate basis. Such loans allow the interest rate charges to change according to market conditions. If current rates are high, you'll pay more in interest fees, when rates go down, your interest costs will drop too.

In a way, student loans can be described as variable-rate loans from the lender's point of view because of the special allowance feature. One of the more attractive aspects of these loans, to the borrower, is their reasonable interest rates. However, from the lender's view, tying up money in long-term obligations with fixed rates of seven percent to nine percent isn't good business.

To encourage lenders to participate in the GSLP and make low interest loans, the federal government developed the idea of "special allowance." This is a fee paid to GSLP lenders each quarter to help compensate them for the lower interest rates charged to student borrowers.

Calculation of the special allowance fee takes into consideration present money market conditions. Rates for special allowance payments are calculated each quarter by averaging the bond-equivalent rates on the previous 91 days' Treasury Bill yields. To this average, an allowance or "spread" of 3.25 percent is added. This result is the total yield on the student loan for the quarter. The student loan's interest rate (that rate appearing on the borrower's Promissory Note) represents the subsidy portion of the yield. This is subtracted from that total yield calculation, above, and the difference represents the special allowance. If the loan yield to the lender is 12 percent, then the subsidy on an eight percent GSL is eight percent, and the special allowance is four percent. All rates are expressed in annual terms. The 1986 Higher Education Amendments capped lenders' yields at 10 percent for GSLs and 12.75 percent for PLUS loans.

The Consolidated Omnibus Budget Reconciliation Act of 1985, popularly known as "Graham-Rudman" has also had an effect on the special allowance. Through a mechanism known as a "Presidential Sequester Order," the special allowance on all loans disbursed after March 1, 1986, will be lowered to 3.1 percent over the Treasury Bill rate. This reduction takes place for only the first four quarters for those loans disbursed between March and September of 1986.

Obviously special allowance payments can vary with each passing quarter of the year. That's the main idea behind them. The federal government recognized that today's interest market is a variable environment. By making such adjustments in interest paid to lenders, borrowers are afforded with fixed-rate loans at attractive rates while lenders are still fairly compensated from changing market conditions.

Some lenders and secondary markets involved in GSLP activity issue tax-exempt obligations to raise capital for making such loans. These institutions, because they do depend on tax-exempt obligations, receive only one-half of the special allowance rate paid to other lenders.

How Was the 3.25 Percent Decided Upon?

The federal government sees the 3.25 percent as a fair margin to cover servicing costs and costs of funds. Most studies including those prepared for the National Commission on Student Financial Assistance, substantiate that the 3.25 percent margin is a "fair and just return" on a lender's investment in student loans.

Naturally as interest rates rise, the amount that the federal government pays in special allowance also increases. Special allowance payments continue until the loan is fully repaid.

Is it really wise for young borrowers to obligate themselves to lengthy loan commitments?

Any decision to borrow—for education or anything else— must be based on careful and prudent considerations. When you borrow for education, don't let the extended payment terms, or the time before payments begin, charm you into forgetting about the obligation. In previous chapters we strongly encouraged you to seek career advice and judge your potential earnings capacity as you consider borrowing to complete your education. Again, we want to stress the importance of not borrowing more than you can comfortably repay.

An education is one of the most important goals you can pursue. However, it's equally important to achieve it in a manner that will not create undue hardship on you. For example, it may be advisable to borrow less in student loan funds and supplement such monies with part-time employment, even if it means extending your time in school an extra year or more. We've provided information on other aid programs, some of which require no repayments at all. See Chapters 12, 13, 14, 15 and 16 for additional information.

Americans are active users of consumer credit. Our economy and tax structure has to some extent encouraged its use. Credit availability was partly responsible for the post World War II boom in factory output and the resulting rise in prosperity and employment. By tying consumer purchases to installments, timed to their periodic receipt of income, factories could schedule production throughout the months or years. Consumers found that they could satisfy their needs now and meet their obligations from future income, rather that save present income for future wants and needs.

"A bird in hand is worth two in the bush". An old adage? Yes, but applicable when you consider the time value of money. Simply put, money now in hand is more productive than a promise to receive money later. You have the opportunity to use the money now and this use can translate into income, profits, and benefits. A common means to calculate this effect is to discount those future dollars. One means is to use the current market interest rates as the discount rate. If you have a dollar now, you may be able to earn five percent interest on it. If you couldn't have the dollar until one year from now, then you've given up that five percent interest for one year. Your promise of that future dollar is worth approximately 95 cents. You'd have to have 95 cents, approximately, right now to get that whole dollar in one year.

Inflation works in much the same way as the example we just described. As the overall buying power of the dollar drops, the dollars are said to be "cheaper" in comparison with former dollars. In real terms, then, cheaper dollars have less impact on the borrower than dollars that are priced at or are worth face value.

Whenever you promise to give up something later, you retain the use of it now, right? A promise to repay a loan later usually means that you pay with cheaper dollars, since you have had the use of those dollars now. The passing of time usually has a real effect on the real cost of a fixed interest rate. For this reason, the two fixed rates of student loans are attractive to borrowers because they are at a low rate compared to other consumer credit. Their long repayment terms — the maximum is 120 months or ten years — benefit the borrower since the dollars repaid will be "cheaper" as the result of the time value of the money being repaid.

Tax rates and policies also play an important role in consumer debt. If you can deduct the costs of credit (interest), then you, in effect, have a subsidy—or help—in repaying the interest charges. When you itemize income tax returns, you are now allowed to deduct your interest paid. The effect that has on you depends on your income tax bracket. If your tax rate is 25 percent, then you can switch $1 of taxable income from any tax liability for each $4 of interest paid. In other words, the interest paid is being subsidized by the tax rates. It is the same as if the IRS was simply paying one-fourth, in this example, of your borrowing costs. Significant changes were also made to the tax code in 1986. Many of the usual itemized deductions were changed. Only the deductibility of interest on mortgage debt incurred for education has remained.

Careful use of credit is important to your future. All student loans, as well as regular consumer credit transactions, become part of your active credit file. Be sure to consider all aspects of debt before obligating yourself. Our best advice? If you do borrow, borrow wisely.

Chapter 9

Where to Apply for Your Loan

It's easy to apply for a GSL. More than likely there are several places in your own community or at least close by participating in the GSLP.

Many lending institutions throughout the United States are committed to providing financial aid to students pursuing educational goals. They believe it is a wise investment in our country's future. Lending institutions realize that without such programs as the GSLP, millions of students would find it extremely difficult if not impossible to adequately meet the skyrocketing costs associated with a postsecondary education.

State and private agencies are the most popular source of student loan funds. Approximately 13,000 financial institutions participate in the GSLP. Most of these institutions are national and state banks, credit unions, or federal savings & loan associations. If your community lender does not participate, they may be able to refer you to another institution.

State agencies, along with private, non-profit guarantee agencies, may be authorized to act as GSLP lenders. In most cases, these lending activities are undertaken only as a last resort. They may permit limited lending functions, but only if there are no other commercial sources for the GSLP.

Most schools and colleges have a ready outlet for their student loan applications. Since most applications originate or pass through a college's Financial Aid Office, the college usually has a list available of the active lenders and sources of GSLP loans. Some colleges make a practice of referring all applications to a specific lender unless the student has his own participating lender.

You should have no difficulty finding a source for the loan. That's really the easy part! Be sure to act early and work on getting your projected budget, school location, and loan eligibility established. After this has been completed, you'll likely have the names of several willing lenders.

If you visit a lender in person, you may be more successful in getting a loan than when inquiring by telephone or letter only. It's best if you can establish personal communication with your lender. You'll find, also, that the bankers are usually more than willing to discuss your borrowing options and needs. If you are unsuccessful at finding a lender, contact the guarantee agency for your state. Refer to Appendix A for a listing of all state and designated guarantee agencies.

Chapter 10

The Service Agency's Role

A service agency helps to support recordkeeping activities associated with student and parent loans. Service-related functions include receiving monthly loan payments, collecting past due accounts, tracking borrowers while in school to ensure on-going compliance with eligibility terms, and billing borrowers when loan payments are due.

Did you notice that nowhere did we mention the disbursement of loans?

Lending institutions make loans. Service agencies support loans. However, a lending institution may also act as a service agency. On the other hand, a lending institution may (and often does) sell its loans to a service agency or contracts with that agency for support purposes. In such cases, all the lender does is process applications and make credit decisions. In some cases, the service agency disburses the loan proceeds, after lender approval, out of an account set up expressly for this purpose. These arrangements are made in order to reduce the handling of the application and time on the financial institution's part.

When a service agency is involved, the borrower does not make payments directly to the lender. For example, Main Street Bank may have accepted your application, determined your eligibility for credit, arranged for insurance by the guarantee agency, and disbursed the proceeds. Once payment begins, however, you may be writing your monthly checks to the XYZ Service Corporation.

The above illustration is the most common example of how the borrower interacts with a service agency. The lenders may contract with a servicer to carry out billing and collection functions, or they may actually sell their loan portfolio to an organization commonly referred to as a "secondary marketer." Sallie Mae, a corporation we're going to discuss later in this chapter, is one of the better known secondary marketers for GSLs.

A secondary marketer assumes all responsibility for collecting the outstanding principal and interest on loans purchased. Both lenders and secondary marketers may contract with private service agencies that perform billing and/or collection activities. For the rendering of such services, the service agency charges the lender or owner a fee or percentage of the revenue collected.

Why do so many lenders enter into service agency agreements or sell their portfolios to secondary marketers?

The main reason why some GSL lenders do not follow the GSL loan through repayment is one of cost. Since this particular type of loan represents a very small percentage of the institution's total lending operation, high costs will more than likely be associated with the servicing of GSLs. It's often more profitable to sell or contract for servicing them rather than for a lender to independently handle all support functions.

When a loan servicer is used, the fees are usually based on the borrower, not on the loan. That means that a borrower with more than one loan costs the lender the same service fee as the borrower with only one loan.

A lender that sells loans outright does so to accomplish two things. First, this frees up capital which can be used to originate more student loans. Even with special allowances and guarantees, many lenders wish to limit their participation in the GSL program. Second, this sale does not tie the lender to holding and servicing or contracting for service throughout the loan repayment. Holding a student loan from disbursement through repayment can be a longer obligation that the lender wants.

As a GSLP borrower, you do have certain legal rights when your loan is sold or involved with a servicer. If the lender sells or transfers the right to receive payments to a third party, you must be notified. The seller will tell you who to contact for loan information or when making payments. The guarantor and the Department of Education are both advised. The guarantor needs to know who holds the loans being insured, and the DOE must know to whom the interest payments belong.

Sallie Mae

Sallie Mae, or S.L.M.A., is an acronym for the Student Loan Marketing Association. It is by far the best known secondary market for GSL's.

Sallie Mae began operations in 1973. A key participant in the GSLP, its primary purpose is to serve as the national secondary market for GSL's. This is a government chartered stockholder-owned corporation. Broad statutory authority has been granted to Sallie Mae by Congress in order to assure a sound national secondary market and sufficient liquidity and funding for the GSLP. Corporate activities are overseen by a board of directors. This board differs from most public and private institutions because it contains members appointed by the President and members who are representing educational institutions and financial institutions.

One way to describe Sallie Mae is to say that it serves as a "lender's bank". Liquidity is provided to lending institutions participating in the GSLP by:

1. Purchase of GSL's from lenders.

2. Making "warehousing advances" (short-term loans to lenders secured by the lender's own student loan inventory).

In addition, Sallie Mae offers services related to state student loan revenue bonds and student lending under the Health Education Assistance Loan (HEAL) program.

Sallie Mae has recently been active in developing and marketing automated servicing programs for lenders and new parent loan programs.

For more information on Sallie Mae and the programs they offer, you may contact:

Student Loan Marketing Association
1055 Thomas Jefferson Street, N.W.
Washington, DC 20007

Chapter 11

The Future
for the GSLP

During recent years, federal lawmakers have been placing greater emphasis on finding ways to reduce federal spending for the GSL programs.

We previously mentioned the Graham-Rudman legislation and its 1986-87 budget balancing effort. In addition to these changes, the student loan program periodically comes before Congress for renewal or reauthorization. When this happens, Congress usually takes this opportunity to change the program.

The reauthorization process was completed during the 99th Congress. Legislation making rather sweeping changes was signed into law by President Reagan on October 17, 1986. The changes brought about in this legislation will touch each of you for several years to come. More important, there continues to be an urgent need of the government to control spending and deficits. Student financial aid programs will likely be the target of further cuts.

We cannot anticipate the form of future change. Yields to lenders will be reviewed with further cuts in mind. The needs tests and ways of measuring "Family Contribution" will also be monitored. You can be certain that if the family of tomorrow's children are able to support some portion of the costs of education, they will be expected to bear that commitment. For these reasons, the chapters on alternative money sources and financial planning are extremely important to you and your parents.

Just as parents are expected to pay their fair share, the student will be required to provide more support for the program, thus reducing the federal government's role. One way is by allowing the student interest rates to increase to rates nearer with market rates. This will ensure the appropriate yield for the lenders and reduce the costs to the government. This will, however, increase the costs to the student. Students must plan carefully for their education and not ignore the effects of larger payments on their take-home incomes.

Many changes to these government-supported programs only apply to new students. However, even this rule is changing. Now many of the new policies and procedures will apply equally to the new GSLP borrower and to existing ones. One important note. As you progress through your education and through repayment of student debt, keep yourself informed of the policy changes. You might be surprised to discover that new rules may affect debts incurred several years ago.

Chapter 12

The Pell Grant

Pell Grants do not have to be repaid. As its name implies, this particular form of financial aid is a grant. If you get one, so much the better. You'll be way ahead when it comes to paying for a postsecondary education.

Sounds like a good idea, right?

If you qualify for one, a Pell Grant is great. However, please note that you must qualify. A grant that does not have to be repaid is not something that the government could afford to offer to everyone without qualification.

Not every student can get a Pell Grant. There are two very important conditions attached to these grants.

1. You must be an undergraduate student.

2. Financial need must be present.

The first stipulation is easy to explain. You can't be a graduate student. Only students working on undergraduate degrees or programs may apply for Pell Grants.

The second condition–financial need–is considerably more complicated to explain. A standard formula is used by the U.S. Department of Education to determine eligibility. Congress revises and approves this formula every year. Called the Pell Grant Methodology, it establishes both eligibility and the amount of the grant.

The needs analysis process for a Pell Grant is very similar to that for the GSLP. You may want to obtain a calculation guidebook which will provide a line-by-line example of the Pell needs analysis, as well as sample forms which you may use to calculate your own SAI. For a free copy write to:

Formula Book
Department DED-87
Pueblo, CO 81009

For the 1985-86 academic year, the maximum Pell Grant

awarded to a student was $2,100. The amount of available money depends on how much funding Congress gives the program. Nearly $4 billion will be distributed during the 1987-88 academic year. Grants are expected to range from $200 to $2,300, or 60 percent of the school's attendance costs, whichever is less.

Did you notice how great the range is for a Pell Grant? There's a considerable difference between $200 and $2,300.

Part of what the Pell Grant Methodology does is determine your expected family contribution. Income, number of dependents, and assets are examples of the criteria used for this process. For example, a family of four with an annual income of $30,000 and assets of $25,000 is expected to contribute more than the same size family with an annual income of $25,000 and assets of $15,000.

The more your family is judged "capable" of contributing, the smaller the grant. The smaller their contribution, the bigger the grant.

Under the Pell Grant Methodology, expected family contribution can be large enough to exclude you from qualifying for a grant. The formula assigns each applicant a "Student Aid Index" (SAI). This number appears on your Student Aid Report (SAR) once it is successfully processed and returned to you. For more information on the SAR, refer to Appendix A – Student Aid Report.

Does the Student Aid Report and the SAI tell you how much of a grant you qualify for? No, it can't because other factors besides personal finances must be considered. Cost of education, enrollment status and length of attendance all influence the amount of an award. For example, half-time students receive only 50 percent of the award amount.

The same family case histories that we used for the GSLP needs analysis may be used again to demonstrate the Pell SAI calculations. Family E was a family of three, a single parent, with one child seeking financial aid. The Pell formula will calculate an expected contribution from parental income and assets and from the students' income and assets.

On line 1 enter adjusted gross income from IRS Form 1040-line 32, 1040A-line 14 or 1040-EZ line 3. Separately list the father's and mother's incomes, even if they do not add up to the amount shown in the total on line 1. This discrepancy sometimes occurs since there may have been adjustments to one of the parents' income due to employee business expenses, payments to an IRA or the addition of taxable pensions.

From Tax Return	Line 1.	25,000
Earned from work by father	Line 1a.	25,000
Earned from work by mother	Line 1b.	
Deduction for married couple when both work	Line 2.	0
Untaxed Social Security benefits to parents	Line 3.	0
Last year's benefits paid for AFDC or ADC	Line 4.	0
Parents' other untaxed income	Line 5.	0
One half of this year's expected VA benefits if any paid to student	Line 6.	0
Sum of lines 1 thru 6	Line 7.	25,000
Subtract the Federal Income tax paid	Line 8.	-3,000
Balance remaining is effective family income	Line 9.	22,000

Offsets are deducted from effective income

Family Size Offset (see Table 1)	Line 10.	7,800
Medical Expenses if over 20% of effective income	Line 11.	0
Employment expense (see Table 2)	Line 12.	1,500
Unreimbursed elementary and Secondary school tuition	Line 13.	0
Total offset sum Lines 10 thru 13	Line 14.	9,300
Discretionary income Line 9 minus Line 14	Line 15.	12,700
Standard Contribution from Family Income — See Table 3	Line 16.	1,686

Asset Contribution

Value of residence if owned	Line 17.	25,000
The first 25,000 of value of owned residence is reserved from consideration	Line 18.	-25,000
Available parental home assets — Subtract line 18 from 17, if negative or 0 enter 0	Line 19.	0
Parents' other assets cost, savings, other investments	Line 20.	2,000
The first 25,000 of asset value is reserved from consideration	Line 21.	25,000
Total other assets — Subtract Line 21 from Line 20, if negative or 0 enter 0	Line 22.	0
Add Lines 19 and 22. This total is available parental assets	Line 23.	0
Standard contribution from total available parental assets, if Line 23 is positive multiply it by .05; otherwise enter 0	Line 24.	0

If Line 15 is negative enter here as a positive number,
otherwise enter 0 — Line 25.   0

Contribution from parental assets Line 24 minus Line
25 enter if positive or zero. Line 26a enter negative
amount from Line 26 — Line 26.   0

Contribution from Family Income and Parental Assets.
Add Line 16 and Line 26 — Line 27.   1,686

Multiple student adjustment rate (See Table 3) — Line 28.   100%

Multiply Line 27 by rate on Line 28 and enter here.
This is adjusted parental contribution from income
and assets — Line 29.   1,686

The next steps will calculate the student's portion of the SAI.

Net assets of student — Line 30.   500

Available assets — first 25,000 of assets are
protected — Line 31.   -25,000

Contribution from student's assets — Multiply Line
31 by .33 if single student, .05 if married
Student's Income and Offsets — Line 32.   0

Student's taxable income — Line 33.   900

Student's income tax paid — Line 34.   0

Net income Line 33 minus Line 34 — Line 35.   900

Add student's untaxed income — Line 36.   0

Student total income add Line 35 and Line 36
For next year's comparison, multiply Line 37 by .60
and enter results 37R 540 — Line 37.   900

Next fiscal year estimated income July 1 to June 30 — Line 38.   900

Effective income, if Line 38 is greater than 37R, enter
amount from line 37 here. If 37R is greater than or
equal to Line 38, enter amount from Line 38 here — Line 39.   900

Offset for negative parental income enter negative
amount, if any, from Line 26R — Line 40.   0

Dependent student offset; single student = 3,400
married student = 5,100 — Line 41.   3,400

Total offset Line 40 plus Line 41 — Line 42.   3,400

Student discretionary income. Line 39 minus Line 42 — Line 43.   -2,500

Contribution from student income. If Line 43 is
positive, multiply it by .75 if the student is single, .25 if
the student is married. If Line 43 is negative or 0,
enter 0 on Line 44. — Line 44.   0

Student Aid Index = the sum of lines 29, 32 and 44. — Line 45.   1,686

This is the result using the Family E case originally presented in Chapter 6—The Needs Test. Blank worksheets are included at the end of this chapter. You may use them when calculating your own SAI estimate. If your family has business or farm income and assets, please note that there are separate worksheets to be used.

The following information centers can provide you with additional information on Pell Grants. Also, they can provide assistance on filling out the SAR and tell you whether or not your application has been processed. But please don't try to make collect calls. Neither will accept the charges. You are the one wanting the information, so it's your responsibility to pay the telephone charges.

Application Processing Center
(319) 337-3738
Iowa City, Iowa

9:00 a.m. until 7:00 p.m.
(Eastern Standard Time)
Monday through Friday

Federal Student Aid Information Center
(301) 984-4070
Rockville, MD

9:00 a.m. until 5:30 p.m.
Eastern Standard Time
Monday through Friday

Congress established the Pell Grant program in 1972, originally calling it the Basic Educational Opportunity Grant Program. Based solely on financial need, this was the first form of federal student aid ever to be awarded directly to the student. Today the Pell Grant Program is the largest student aid program funded solely with federal dollars.

How Do You Apply For A Pell?

It's really very simple! All you have to do is file a Student Aid Report (SAR).

Application for a Pell Grant can be made immediately after January 1 of the year in which you plan to attend college. For example, if you plan to start college in September of 1988, apply as soon as possible after January 1, 1988. The sooner you do, the better.

If you're eligible for a Pell Grant, the SAR returned to you by the processing center has three parts. If you are not eligible, the report will consist of only two parts.

The information used to determine eligibility is contained in Part 2 of the SAR. Review this information very carefully. If the processor made an error, contact the processor immediately.

If the document is error free, sign the SAR. A photocopy of both sides of Part 1 must be sent to the financial aid administrator of each school where application is being made.

Once you finalize your decision regarding the school to attend, send all three parts of the SAR to that school's financial aid administrator. The administrator will then use the Student Aid Index (SAI) number to determine the actual amount of your grant.

All applications must be validated by the school's financial aid administrator. At this time you will be required to produce income tax forms and other related documents. The purpose of these reviews is to validate the information you've provided to ensure that all applications are accurately complete. The federal government will revalidate more than one million of these applications. Because of these checks and reviews, it is important to be truthful when completing the SAR. Incorrect answers may jeopardize your award.

What if something drastically changes your personal finances after filing an SAR? Conditions such as divorce and death can significantly effect family finances. Another form called the "Special Condition Application" was designed for this specific purpose. Talk with your high school counselor or financial aid administrator if such a need arises.

How Is Pell Paid?

Each school that participates in the Pell Grant program is guaranteed funds by the U.S. Department of Education. These schools receive enough money to pay all Pell Grants awarded to their students.

Usually a school will pay you in one of the following ways:

1. Credit your account,

2. Pay you the money directly, or

3. A combination of the first two methods.

Every student receiving a Pell Grant must be informed in writing how much the award will be along with how and when the money will be paid. Congress also requires participating schools to pay these grants at least once per term (i.e. semester, quarter). If a school does not have traditional terms, then payments must be made at least twice per academic year.

The Alternate Disbursement System (ADS) is a payment methodology used by some schools. The federal government issues checks directly to the student for their award proceeds. To get a check, however, you are required to fill out a "Request for Payment of Award" (Form 304). If you attend a school which uses this payment system, ask your financial aid administrator about this form.

Approximately four to six weeks after the form is mailed in, you will receive an "ADS Student Report" (Form 304-1). This form tells you how much the first award will be.

Are subsequent payments automatically made? No. In order to get any remaining grant money, you must file another "ADS Student Report." This document tells when and how to go about the process. Like all other aspects of the Pell Grant program, it can be revised by Congress from time to time.

What If You Transfer?

Your Pell Grant money won't suddenly disappear just because you transfer–as long as you do one simple thing. Get a duplicate of your Student Aid Report (SAR), and then submit it to the financial aid administrator at the new school you've selected. That's all there is to it.

Should You Apply For A Pell Even If You Are Not Eligible?

Yes. It's very important that you do so. The schools as well as the state agencies expect you to apply for a Pell Grant. It's also a prerequisite to eligibility for a GSL. Unless you've been turned down for a Pell Grant, most private and state sources of financial aid will not even consider your application.

Summary

Pell Grants are great! If you qualify, they are free money with no strings attached. For thousands of students, Pells provide a solid foundation for a financial aid package. Aid from other federal and non-federal sources is often added to Pell money in order to cover fully the cost of an education. Good examples are GSL, NDSL or scholarships.

TABLE 1. Family Size Offsets

Family Size	Dollar Amounts
2	$ 6,400
3	7,800
4	9,900
5	11,800
6	13,200
More than 6	$1,600 each addition

TABLE 2. Offset for Employment

When both parents work, the offset amounts to:

50% of the earnings of the parent with the lowest earnings or $1,500, whichever is lower;

For a single parent family, the offset is 50% of the earnings of that parent or $1,500, whichever is less.

TABLE 3. Expected Contribution From Discretionary Family Income

Discretionary Income	Expected Contribution
$0 to $5,,000	11% of Discretionary Income
$5,001 to $10,000	$550 + 13% of amount over $5,000
$10,001 to $15,000	$1,200 + 18% of amount over 10,000
$15,001 and above	$2,100 + 25% of amount over $15,000

TABLE 4. Multiple Student Adjustment Table

Number of Family Members Enrolled in Postsecondary Education	Contribution per Student as a Percent of Standard Contribution
1	100%
2	70%
3	50%
4 or more	40%

WORKSHEET A

1987-88 STUDENT AID INDEX
DEPENDENT STUDENT FORMULA
(NO FARM/BUSINESS ASSETS)

FAMILY INCOME AND OFFSETS

1. Parents' 1986 income from IRS Form 1040-line 32, 1040A-line 14, or 1040EZ-line 3. See instructions.

   a. Amount earned from work by father.
   b. Amount earned from work by mother.

2. Parents' 1986 deduction for a married couple when both work. See instructions. ✧

3. Parents' 1986 Social Security benefits. ✧

4. Parents' 1986 benefits from Aid to Families with Dependent Children - AFDC or ADC ✧

5. Parents' other untaxed income and benefits for 1986. See instructions. ✧

6. One-half of the student's expected veterans educational benefits. ✧

7. Annual adjusted family income in 1986. (Lines 1 + 2 + 3 + 4 + 5 + 6). ⊜

8. Parents' 1986 U.S. income tax paid or payable. ▱

9. Effective family income in 1986. (Line 7 minus line 8) ⊜

10. Family size offset (Table 1). ✧
11. Offset for unusual medical expenses. ✧
12. Offset for employment expense. ✧
13. Offset for unreimbursed elementary and secondary school tuition and fees. ✧
14. Total offset against income. (Lines 10 + 11 + 12 + 13) ⊜

15. Student's (and spouse's) discretionary family income (line 9 minus line 14). ⊜

16. **Contribution from Family Income** Find amount from Table 2 (if line 15 is 0 or a negative number, enter 0 on line 16).

PARENTS' ASSETS/RESERVES

17. Net value of parents' residence, if owned.

18. Asset reserve for residence. ▱ **25,000**

19. Available parental home assets (line 17 - line 18). If negative or 0, enter 0. ⊜

20. Parents' other net assets: cash, savings and checking accounts; other real estate/investments. See instructions.

21. Asset reserve for other net assets. ▱ **25,000**

22. Other available parental assets (line 20 - line 21). If negative or 0, enter 0. ⊜

23. Parents' total available assets (line 19 + 22).

    Assessment rate **x .05**

24. Standard contribution from total available assets. (If line 23 is negative or 0, enter 0). ⊜

25. Offset for negative discretionary income. (if line 15 is negative, enter it as a positive number, otherwise enter 0). ▱

26. **Contribution from Parents' Assets**
    (Line 24 minus line 25; if result is positive or 0, enter on line 26; if result is negative, enter in box 26R.
    26R

27. Contribution from family income and parents' assets (line 16 + line 26). ✧

28. Multiple Student Adjustment Rate (Table 3) ⊠

29. **Parental contribution from income and assets**

STUDENT'S ASSETS/RESERVES

30. Net assets of student (and spouse).

31. Student's (and spouse's) available assets.
    o If the student is married, subtract 25,000
    from the amount on line 30.
    If positive, enter the result
    on line 31. If the result is negative or 0,
    enter 0 on line 31.

    - 25,000

    o If the student is single, enter the amount
    from line 30 on line 31.

Assessment Rate
(Multiply line 31 by .33 for a single
student; by .05 for a married student)

**32. Contribution from
Student Assets**

STUDENT'S INCOME/OFFSETS

33. Student's (and spouse's) taxable income
for 1986. See instructions.

34. Student's (and spouse's) U.S. income
tax paid or payable for 1986.　o

35. Student's (and spouse's) taxable income
for 1986, after U. S. income tax
(line 33 - line 34).　≋

36. Student's (and spouse's) untaxed income
and benefits for 1986. See instructions.　✧

37. Student's (and spouse's) total 1986 income
(line 35 + line 36).　≋
Multiply line 37 by
.60 and enter result
on line 37R.
37R

x .60

38. Student's (and spouse's) estimated
1987-88 income (July 1, 1987 - June 30, 1988).

39. Student's (and spouse's) effective income.
If line 38 is greater than 37R, enter amount
from line 37 here. If line 37R is greater than
or equal to line 38, enter amount from line 38.

40. Offset for negative parental income that is
not used as an offset against asset
contribution. Enter negative amount,
if any , from line 26R as a positive
number here.

41. Dependent student offset.
(single student = $3500
married student = $5200)　✧

42. Total offset against student's income
(line 40 + line 41).　≋

43. Student's (and spouse's) discretionary
income (line 39 - line 42).　≋

Assessment Rate
(multiply line 43 by .75 for a single student,
or by .25 for a married student; if line 43
is negative or 0, enter 0 on line 44)

**44. Contribution from
Student Income**

45. Student Aid Index
(line 29 + line 32 + line 44)

1987-88 STUDENT AID INDEX

DEPENDENT STUDENT FORMULA
(WITH FARM/BUSINESS ASSETS)

FAMILY INCOME AND OFFSETS

1. Parents' 1986 income from IRS Form 1040-line 32, 1040A-line 14, or 1040EZ-line 3. See instructions.

    a. Amount earned from work by father.

    b. Amount earned from work by mother.

2. Parents' 1986 deduction for a married couple when both work. See instructions. ✛

3. Parents' 1986 Social Security benefits. ✛

4. Parents' 1986 benefits from Aid to Families with Dependent Children - AFDC or ADC ✛

5. Parents' other untaxed income and benefits for 1986. See instructions. ✛

6. One-half of the student's expected veterans educational benefits. ✛

7. Annual adjusted family income in 1986. (Lines 1 + 2 + 3 + 4 + 5 + 6). ≋

8. Parents' 1986 U.S. income tax paid or payable. ▫

9. Effective family income in 1986 (line 7 minus line 8). ≋

10. Family size offset (Table 1). ✛

11. Offset for unusual medical expenses. ✛

12. Offset for employment expense. ✛

13. Offset for unreimbursed elementary and secondary school tuition and fees. ✛

14. Total offset against income. (Lines 10 + 11 + 12 + 13) ≋

15. Student's (and spouse's) discretionary family income (line 9 minus line 14). ≋

16. **Contribution from Family Income** Find amount from Table 2 (if line 15 is 0 or a negative number, enter 0 on line 16).

PARENTS' ASSETS/RESERVES

17a. Net value of parents' residence, if owned.

17b. Asset reserve for residence. Enter 25,000 or the net home asset from line 17a, whichever is less. ▫

17c. Available parental home assets (line 17a - line 17b). If negative or 0, enter 0. ≋

18a. Parents' other net assets: cash, savings and checking accounts; other real estate/investments. See instructions.

18b. Asset reserve for other net assets. Enter 25,000 or the value of of other net assets from line 18a, whichever is less. ▫

18c. Other available parental assets (line 18a - line 18b). If negative or 0, enter 0. ≋

19. Maximum allowable asset reserve for all parental assets. `100,000`

20. Total asset reserve already used (line 17b + line 18b). ▫

21. Remaining available asset reserve (line 19 - line 20). ≋

22a. Parents' net farm and business assets.

22b. Asset reserve for farm and business assets. Enter one of the following amounts, whichever is least: ▫

   o 80,000, or
   o the remaining available asset reserve from line 21, or
   o the net value of farm/business assets from line 22a.

22c. Available farm and business assets (line 22a - line 22b).

23. Total available parental assets (lines 17c + 18c + 22c).

24. Standard contribution from total available parental assets. If line 23 is negative or 0, enter 0 here. **x .05**

25. Offset for negative discretionary income. (If line 15 is negative, enter it as a positive number, otherwise enter 0.)

26. **Contribution from Parents' Assets**
(Line 24 minus line 25; if result is positive or 0, enter on line 26; if result is negative, enter in box 26R.
26R

27. Contribution from family income and parental assets (line 16 + line 26).

28. Multiple student adjustment rate (Table 3).

29. **Parental contribution from income and assets**

STUDENT'S ASSETS/RESERVES

30. Net assets of student (and spouse).

31. Student's (and spouse's) available assets.
o If the student is married, subtract 25,000 from the amount on line 30. If positive, enter the result on line 31. If the result is negative or 0, enter 0 on line 31. **25,000**

o If the student is single, enter the amount from line 30 on line 31.

Assessment Rate
(Multiply line 31 by .33 for a single student; by .05 for a married student)

32. **Contribution from Student Assets**

STUDENT'S INCOME/OFFSETS

33. Student's (and spouse's) taxable income for 1986. See instructions.

34. Student's (and spouse's) U.S. income tax paid or payable for 1986.

35. Student's (and spouse's) taxable income for 1986, after U. S. income tax. (Line 33 - line 34).

36. Student's (and spouse's) untaxed income and benefits for 1986. See instructions.

37. Student's (and spouse's) total 1986 income (line 35 + line 36).
Multiply line 37 by .60 and enter result on line 37R. **x .60**
37R

38. Student's (and spouse's) estimated 1987-88 income (July 1, 1987 -June 30, 1988).

39. Student's (and spouse's) effective income. If line 38 is greater than 37R, enter amount from line 37 here. If line 37R is greater than or equal to line 38, enter amount from line 38.

40. Offset for negative parental income that is not used as an offset against asset contribution. Enter negative amount, if any , from line 26R as a positive number here.

41. Dependent student offset. (single student = $3500 married student = $5200)

42. Total offset against student's income (line 40 + line 41).

43. Student's (and spouse's) discretionary income (line 39 - line 42).

Assessment Rate
(multiply line 43 by .75 for a single student, or by .25 for a married student; if line 43 is negative or 0, enter 0 on line 44)

44. **Contribution from Student Income**

45. **Student Aid Index**
(line 29 + line 32 + line 44)

1987-88 STUDENT AID INDEX
INDEPENDENT STUDENT FORMULA
(FAMILY SIZE OF ONE)

WORKSHEET C

INCOME AND OFFSETS

1. Student's 1986 income from IRS Form 1040-line 32, 1040A-line 14, or 1040EZ-line 3. See instructions.

2. Student's 1986 Social Security benefits. ⊹

3. Student's other untaxed income and benefits for 1986. See instructions. ⊹

4. One-half of the student's expected veterans educational benefits. ⊹

5. Annual adjusted family income in 1986. (Lines 1 + 2 + 3 + 4.) ≋

6. Student's 1986 U.S. income tax paid or payable. ▫

7. Effective family income in 1986. (Line 5 minus line 6) ≋

8. Family size offset (Table 1). **5,200**

9. Offset for unusual medical expenses. ⊹

10. Total offset against income (line 8 + line 9). ≋

11. Student's discretionary income. (Line 7 minus line 10.) ≋

Assessment Rate
(if line 11 is 0 or a negative number, enter 0 on line 12.) **x .75**

12. **Contribution from Student's Income**

ASSET INFORMATION

13. Student's net assets.

Assessment rate **x .33**

14. Standard contribution from student's assets. ≋

15. Offset for negative discretionary income. (If line 11 is negative, enter it as a positive number; otherwise enter 0.) ▫

16. **Contribution from Student's Assets** (Line 14 minus line 15; if result is negative or 0, enter 0.)

17. **Student Aid Index** (Sum of lines 12 and 16.)

WORKSHEET D

1987-88 STUDENT AID INDEX
INDEPENDENT STUDENT FORMULA
(FAMILY SIZE GREATER THAN ONE)

INCOME AND OFFSETS

1. Student's (and spouse's) 1986 income from IRS Form 1040-line 32, 1040A-line 14, or 1040EZ-line 3. See instructions.

   a. Amount earned from work by student.
   b. Amount earned from work by spouse.

2. Student's (and spouse's) 1986 deduction for a married couple when both work. See instructions. ✧

3. Student's (and spouse's) 1986 Social Security benefits. ✧

4. Student's (and spouse's) 1986 benefits from Aid to Families with Dependent Children - AFDC or ADC ✧

5. Student's other untaxed income and benefits for 1986. See instructions. ✧

6. One-half of the student's expected veterans educational benefits. ✧

7. Annual adjusted family income in 1986. (Lines 1 + 2 + 3 + 4 + 5 + 6) ≋

8. Student's (and spouse's) 1986 U.S. income tax paid or payable. ⌀

9. Effective family income in 1986. (Line 7 minus line 8) ≋

10. Family size offset (Table 1). ✧
11. Offset for unusual medical expenses. ✧
12. Offset for employment expense. ✧
13. Offset for unreimbursed elementary and secondary school tuition and fees. ✧
14. Total offset against income. (Lines 10 + 11 + 12 + 13) ≋

15. Student's (and spouse's) discretionary family income (line 9 minus line 14). ≋

Assessment Rate
(if line 15 is 0 or a negative number, enter 0 on line 16) **x .25**

16. **Contribution from Student's (and Spouse's) Income**

ASSET INFORMATION

17. Net value of student's (and spouse's) residence, if owned.

18. Asset reserve for residence. ⌀ **25,000**

19. Available home assets (line 17 - line 18). If negative or 0, enter 0. ≋

20. Student's (and spouse's) other net assets: cash, savings and checking accounts; other real estate/investments. See instructions.
21. Asset reserve for other net assets. ⌀ **25,000**
22. Other available assets (line 20 - line 21). If negative or 0, enter 0.

23. Total available assets (line 19 + line 22). ≋

   Assessment rate **x .05**

24. Standard contribution from total available assets. (If line 23 is negative or 0, enter 0). ≋

25. Offset for negative discretionary income. (if line 15 is negative, enter it as a positive number, otherwise enter 0). ⌀

26. **Contribution from Student's (and Spouse's) Assets** (Line 24 minus line 25; if result is negative or 0, enter 0)

27. Contribution from income and assets (line 16 + line 26). ≋

28. Multiple Student Adjustment Rate (Table 3). 𝕏

29. Adjusted contribution from income (line 27 x line 28). ≋

30. **Student Aid Index** = line 29

WORKSHEET D

1987-88 STUDENT AID INDEX
INDEPENDENT STUDENT FORMULA
(FAMILY SIZE GREATER THAN ONE)

INCOME AND OFFSETS

1. Student's (and spouse's) 1986 income from IRS Form 1040-line 32, 1040A-line 14, or 1040EZ-line 3. See instructions.

   a. Amount earned from work by student.

   b. Amount earned from work by spouse.

2. Student's (and spouse's) 1986 deduction for a married couple when both work. See instructions. ✧

3. Student's (and spouse's) 1986 Social Security benefits. ✧

4. Student's (and spouse's) 1986 benefits from Aid to Families with Dependent Children - AFDC or ADC ✧

5. Student's other untaxed income and benefits for 1986. See instructions. ✧

6. One-half of the student's expected veterans educational benefits. ✧

7. Annual adjusted family income in 1986. (Lines 1 + 2 + 3 + 4 + 5 + 6) ☰

8. Student's (and spouse's) 1986 U.S. income tax paid or payable. ▫

9. Effective family income in 1986. (Line 7 minus line 8) ☰

10. Family size offset (Table 1). ✧
11. Offset for unusual medical expenses. ✧
12. Offset for employment expense. ✧
13. Offset for unreimbursed elementary and secondary school tuition and fees. ✧
14. Total offset against income. (Lines 10 + 11 + 12 + 13) ☰

15. Student's (and spouse's) discretionary family income (line 9 minus line 14). ☰

Assessment Rate (if line 15 is 0 or a negative number, enter 0 on line 16) **x .25**

16. **Contribution from Student's (and Spouse's) Income**

ASSET INFORMATION

17. Net value of student's (and spouse's) residence, if owned.

18. Asset reserve for residence. ▫ **25,000**

19. Available home assets (line 17 - line 18). If negative or 0, enter 0. ☰

20. Student's (and spouse's) other net assets: cash, savings and checking accounts; other real estate/investments. See instructions.
21. Asset reserve for other net assets. ▫ **25,000**
22. Other available assets (line 20 - line 21). If negative or 0, enter 0.

23. Total available assets (line 19 + line 22). ☰

    Assessment rate **x .05**

24. Standard contribution from total available assets. (If line 23 is negative or 0, enter 0). ☰

25. Offset for negative discretionary income. (if line 15 is negative, enter it as a positive number, otherwise enter 0). ▫

26. **Contribution from Student's (and Spouse's) Assets** (Line 24 minus line 25; if result is negative or 0, enter 0)

27. Contribution from income and assets (line 16 + line 26). ☰

28. Multiple Student Adjustment Rate (Table 3). ✕

29. Adjusted contribution from income (line 27 x line 28). ☰

30. **Student Aid Index** = line 29

WORKSHEET E

1987-88 STUDENT AID INDEX

INDEPENDENT STUDENT FORMULA
(FAMILY SIZE GREATER THAN ONE;
WITH FARM OR BUSINESS ASSETS)

INCOME AND OFFSETS

1. Student's (and spouse's) 1986 income from IRS Form 1040-line 32, 1040A-line 14, or 1040EZ-line 3. See instructions.

   a. Amount earned from work by student.
   b. Amount earned from work by spouse.

2. Student's (and spouse's) 1986 deduction for a married couple when both work. See instructions. ✧

3. Student's (and spouse's) 1986 Social Security benefits. ✧

4. Student's (and spouse's) 1986 benefits from Aid to Families with Dependent Children - AFDC or ADC ✧

5. Student's other untaxed income and benefits for 1986. See instructions. ✧

6. One-half of the student's expected veterans educational benefits. ✧

7. Annual adjusted family income in 1986. (Lines 1 + 2 + 3 + 4 + 5 + 6) ≋

8. Student's (and spouse's) 1986 U.S. income tax paid or payable. ⊖

9. Effective family income in 1986. (Line 7 minus line 8) ≋

10. Family size offset (Table 1). ✧
11. Offset for unusual medical expenses. ✧
12. Offset for employment expense. ✧
13. Offset for unreimbursed elementary and secondary school tuition and fees ✧
14. Total offset against income. (Lines 10+11+12+13) ≋

15. Student's (and spouse's) discretionary family income (line 9 minus line 14). ≋

Assessment Rate
(if line 15 is 0 or a negative number, enter 0 on line 16) **x .25**

16. **Contribution from Student's (and Spouse's) Income**

ASSETS AND RESERVES

17a. Net value of student's (and spouse's) residence, if owned.
17b. Asset reserve for residence. Enter 25,000 or the net home asset (line 17 a), whichever is less. ⊖
17c. Available home assets (line 17a - line 17b). If negative or 0, enter 0. ≋

18a. Student's (and spouse's) other net assets: cash, savings and checking accounts; other real estate/investments. See instructions.
18b. Asset reserve for other net assets. Enter 25,000 or the value of other net assets (line 18a), whichever is less. ⊖
18c. Other available assets (line 18a - line 18b). If negative or 0, enter 0. ≋

19. Maximum allowable reserve for all assets (home, other, farm/ business). **100,000**
20. Total asset reserves already used (line 17b + line 18b) ⊖
21. Remaining available asset reserve (line 19 - line 20). ≋

22a. Student's (and spouse's) net farm and business assets.
22b. Asset reserve for farm and business assets. Enter one of following amounts, whichever is least: ⊖
   o 80,000, or
   o the remaining available asset reserve from line 21, or
   o the net value of farm/business assets from line 22a.

22c. Available farm and business assets (line 22a - line 22b). ≋

ASSETS AND RESERVES (CONT.)

23. Total available assets (line 17c + line 18c + line 22c).	
Assessment rate (If line 23 is 0 or a negative number, enter 0 on line 24.)	x .05
24. Standard contribution from total available assets.	
25. Offset for negative discretionary income. (If line 15 is a negative, enter it as a positive number; otherwise enter 0.)	

26. **Contribution from Student's (and Spouse's) Assets** (Line 24 minus line 25; if result is negative or 0, enter 0.)	

27. Contribution from income and assets (line 16 + line 26).	
28. Multiple Student Adjustment Rate (Table 3)	
29. Adjusted contribution from income (line 27 x line 28).	

30. **Student Aid Index** = line 29	

Chapter 13

Supplemental Educational Opportunity Grant (SEOG)

What's a SEOG?

It's a Supplemental Educational Opportunity Grant. If you're a student though, what's more important is that it's money that doesn't have to be repaid. As its name implies, a SEOG is a grant, not a loan. Only undergraduate students are eligible. The amount awarded is based on the following criteria:

1. Financial need,
2. Availability of funds earmarked for SEOGs at the school you are attending, and
3. The amount of any other financial aid you are receiving.

Eligible students can get up to $2,000 a year. Note that we said "up to." How much you actually get depends on those three qualifying conditions we just listed. Although you might get a SEOG for four consecutive years, the amount can be different each year. Why? Personal finances can change. The total amount of SEOG money distributed by the federal government to your school can increase or decrease along with the number of applicants, thus the average amount available per student can easily fluctuate. Your school's financial aid administrator is the best person to ask about SEOG money and how much is anticipated.

SEOG is a campus-based program. In simple terms, that means that although it's federally funded, it's administered by school personnel. Participating schools receive money for the program from the federal government, and then the school's financial aid administrator distributes it.

When Should I Apply For A SEOG?

It depends on the school you're attending. Different schools have different deadlines. SEOG applications are usually required early in the calendar year. Application for a SEOG must be made each year; these grants are not automatically renewable. Check with your school's financial aid administrator for the deadline, and apply as soon as possible. Each school participating in the SEOG program receives a set amount of money. When the SEOG money is gone, no more grants can be made for that academic year. Now you know why it's best to get your application in as quickly as possible!

How Is A SEOG Paid?

Every student awarded a SEOG is notified in writing by the school's financial aid office. This letter will state the amount awarded, how it will be paid, and may also recap any other financial aid you will be receiving (i.e. scholarships, loans, other grants). Schools usually pay you in one of the following ways:

1. Credit your account.
2. Pay you the money directly.
3. A combination of the above payment methods.

The federal government required participating schools to pay these grants at least once per term (i.e. semester, quarter). If a school does not support formally defined traditional terms, then payments must be made at least twice per academic year.

What If You're Not A Full-Time Student?

Depending on where you attend school, full-time status may not be an eligibility requirement for SEOG money. It's up to the school. For example, some schools allocate 10% of their SEOG funds to part-time students. Check with your school's financial aid administrator for an explanation of their policy.

Summary

SEOGs are one of the best forms of financial aid. Why? Because they are grants, you won't have to repay the money at a later date. SEOGs, like Pell Grants, are often mixed with other forms of financial aid to meet educational expenses. Along with a SEOG, a student aid package may include GSL, NDSL and/ or scholarship monies.

Chapter 14

The Perkins Loan

Money borrowed under the Perkins Loan program must be repaid. That this is a loan and not a grant or gift program is clear from its name. Not only will you have to repay the original amount borrowed, but you are also responsible for paying a certain amount of interest.

This campus-based program is available to both undergraduate and graduate students. Loans made under this program have low interest rates. Currently, the interest rate is five percent. That's great because a low rate means you'll pay out less money for interest. It means more money left in your budget when you start paying off the loan.

Even better, you do not pay interest on the amount borrowed as long as you're in school. Also, interest is not charged to you during deferments or during the six-month grace period that follows each deferment. So in other words, you may have the benefit of Perkins Loan money for several years interest-free. Once you do start making loan payments, the federal government does not recapture the earlier interest. The only interest charge you'll owe is that which accrues on the loan during actual repayment.

The forerunner of this popular program was the National Defense Student Loan program. This program was authorized by Congress in 1958 by the National Defense Education Act. Partly a reaction to the Soviet Union's advances in space exploration, this key piece of legislation established a low-interest loan program for students who could prove financial need. It also established fellowships for graduate students enrolled in certain academic programs, such as the sciences.

Why the space program connection? To review history, the space program created a race between the United States and the Soviet Union. Suddenly there was a demand for more professionals in exciting new fields such as aerospace engineering. Developing the minds of America's youth was one of the best ways Congress knew to meet this challenge. But that took money — more money than most families had. So Congress created a loan program to help meet this financial need.

In 1965 Congress established the National Direct Student Loan program under Title IV-E of the Higher Education Act. This program is a continuation of the National Defense Student Loan Program authorized originally by Title II of the National Defense Education Act of 1958. All rights, privileges, duties, functions, and obligations which existed under the original program continue to exist.

Are Your Eligible For A Perkins Loan?

The Perkins Loan Program is a campus-based program supported by federal dollars. Both undergraduate and graduate students are eligible for Perkins Loans. The amount awarded is based on the following criteria:

1. Financial need.

2. Availability of funds earmarked for Perkins Loans at the school you are attending.

3. The amount of any other financial aid you are receiving.

Even if you qualify, though, there are limitations on the amount you may borrow. From the table below, you can see that the degree level you are pursuing determines the maximum allowed.

LOAN LIMIT	PROGRAM
$ 4,500	Vocational program or completion of less than two years of a program leadning to a bachelor's degree.
$ 9,000	Completion of two years of study toward a bachelor's degree and at least a third-year student status. The $9,000 is minus any Perkins Loan money borrowed previously.
$18,000	Graduate or professional program. This $18,000 is minus any Perkins Loan money borrowed while an undergraduate.

Educational programs approved for Perkins Loans must also meet specific eligibility requirements. These programs must:

1. Admit as regular students only those who:
   a. Have a high school diploma, or
   b. Have a General Educational Development Certificate (GED). A state certificate may be substituted for a GED; the former is issued by some states after the applicant passes an authorized examination. State certificates, like GED's, are recognized as the equivalent of a high school diploma.
   c. Are beyond the age of compulsory school attendance. This can vary among states. For the Perkins Loan program, the applicable age is the same one for the state in which the school is located. Students falling into the category must have the ability to benefit from the education.

2. Offer programs which lead to the following degrees or certificates:
   a. An associate, bachelor, graduate or professional degree.
   b. A two-year program that can be applied for full credit toward a bachelor's degree.
   c. A one-year program leading to a certificate or degree that prepares the student for gainful employment. An example of such a recognized occupation is Electronic Technician.
   d. At least a six-month program leading to a certificate or degree in a proprietary institution or a postsecondary vocational institution. The education offered must prepare the student for gainful employment in a recognized occupation. One example here would be a cosmetology school.

The Perkins Loan is a campus-based program. This means that although the program is federally funded, it's administered by school personnel. Participating schools receive money for the program from the federal government; the school's financial aid administrator then distributes such funds to those applicants who meet eligibility requirements.

Are you automatically guaranteed the maximum available for the degree or certificate program you are pursuing? No. The amount of Perkins Loan money available per applicant at your school can vary from year to year. Furthermore, personal circumstances differ and can influence the true financial need picture of applicants.

Remember how we've previously mentioned "financial aid packages"? Oftentimes, a financial aid administrator uses a Pell Grant award as the main source of funds and supplements the grant money with a Perkins Loan. The types of packages offered should be reviewed with your financial aid administrator as soon as you are accepted for admission.

When Should You Apply For A Perkins Loan?

Get your admission status and finances in order as quickly as possible. It's easier on you and everyone else involved in the process.

The above is the best advice we know regardless of the financial aid program you're interested in. Every school has its own deadline for campus-based programs. Generally speaking, deadlines are early in each calendar year. Check with your school's financial aid administrator for specifics.

How Is A Perkins Loan Paid?

Since a Perkins Loan is a loan, first you have to sign a "promissory note". By signing this legal document, you are agreeing to repay the loan amount, plus any accrued interest. In accordance with the federal guidelines governing this program, a copy of the promissory note and repayment schedule must be given to you.

Students receiving Perkins Loans will be notified by letter from their school's financial aid office. This letter should state the loan amount, how it will be paid, and may also recap any other type of financial aid awarded. Examples of other aids are Pell Grants and scholarships.

Schools usually pay you directly or credit your account for the amount of the Perkins Loan. If your account is credited directly, the school must issue you a receipt. Whichever option is used, the money will be paid to you in at least two payments.

When Does Repayment Start?

A Perkins Loan is a loan, so naturally it must be repaid. Borrowing money for an education is often the first credit transaction ever made by an individual. It's important therefore, to start out on the right foot and honor the obligation. Failure to do so can result in a poor rating on your credit record.

Why is it important to be concerned about your credit record? Because most people need to borrow money from time to time in their lives in order to buy cars, homes, furniture, etc. A bad credit record can hinder your efforts to obtain such funds later in life. If you ask to borrow money, it's your obligation to repay it.

Repayment begins six months after you graduate, leave school, or drop below half-time status. The only exception is if a deferment is granted; more about deferments and the Perkins Loan program shortly.

Up to 10 years may be allowed for repayment. The size of the debt determines the amount of each month's payment. In other words, the more borrowed, the greater the monthly payment owed. Usually at least $30 per month is required regardless of how small the loan.

Can a school demand that you repay the entire amount of a Perkins Loan immediately? Yes. The principal as well as all interest and penalty charges (i.e. for late payments), may be called in by the school at any time for repayment when you have defaulted on the loan. The school can sue you to collect the balance and ask the federal government for assistance in the collection. Along with notifying credit bureaus about the default, the IRS may withhold your income tax refund so that the Perkins Loan debt is collected.

Do Schools Normally Demand Immediate Repayment for the Full Amount of a Perkins Loan?

No. This is definitely the exception. The example mentioned is due to borrower default; that is becoming delinquent in making your monthly payment on time.

What Qualifies Me For A Deferment?

Deferments may be granted for several reasons. When a deferment is granted, the repayment of both principal (the amount you borrowed) and interest are postponed until a later date. Deferment may be granted for up to:

Three Years

1. While you are serving in the military or Public Health Service. You are a Peace Corps volunteer in ACTION programs such as VISTA. Other programs which the Department of Education has determined are comparable to that of ACTION or the Peace Corps may also qualify you for deferment.

2. You or your spouse are temporarily totally disabled. A physician must certify that the disability is both total and temporary.

Two Years

1. While you are serving an internship that is required before professional practice can begin.

One Year

One year deferments are renewable, hardship deferments. In other words, if the qualifying condition persists, deferment may be extended. However, interest does accrue during this type of deferment.

1. Prolonged illness
2. Unemployment
3. Imprisonment

What if you return to school? Perkins Loan payments will be deferred as long as you are enrolled at least half-time in a program approved institution.

Can You Qualify for a Deferment Any Time During the Course of Repayment?

Yes. In fact, you can even qualify for more than one deferment. Any number of deferments may be taken consecutively or at different times during the repayment period. A six-month grace period automatically follows each deferment. So, in reality, if you qualify for a two-year deferment it's actually 30 months before a payment is due again.

Caution! We have discussed deferments as they apply to the GSLP in Chapter 7 — How Repayment Works. The deferment rules for each program are slightly different. The same situation may not qualify for the same deferment or length of deferment for both loans. If you have loans from more than one program, and you believe you may qualify for a deferment, be sure to consult with your lender (or school) for deferment details.

Can My Loan Be Canceled?

Yes. Death or total, permanent disability will cancel a Perkins Loan. In the case of disability, a physician must certify that it is total and permanent.

A Perkins Loan debt can be canceled part by the type of work you do upon leaving school. Part of the debt is canceled for each year you are a full-time teacher of handicapped children. Each year you teach full time in a designated elementary or secondary school that serves low-income students cancels part of a Perkins Loan debt. In both cases, the entire loan is canceled after five years of teaching.

Each year of full-time work in specified Head Start Programs cancels part of a Perkins Loan debt. After seven years of such employment, the entire loan is canceled.

As an enlistment incentive, the Department of Defense will repay a portion of principal owed on a Perkins Loan if you enlist in certain selected specialties of the U.S. Army.

Can I Pay My Loan Off Early?

Yes. You may pay the entire loan balance plus interest due at any time. No penalty is charged for early payoffs.

Your Responsibilities

In addition to eventually paying back the amount borrowed and any interest owed, a Perkins Loan borrower has other responsibilities. You must notify your school if you:

1. Graduate or withdraw from school,
2. Transfer to another school,
3. Drop below half-time status, or
4. Change your name, address, or social security number.

Notification is also required if anything effects your ability to repay the loan. Changes in deferment eligibility or loan cancellation eligibility must also be communicated to school personnel.

Why must the school be provided with this type of information since the Perkins Loan is a federally funded program?

Because it is also a campus-based program. Along with making the loan, the financial aid office is responsible for granting deferments or cancellations. In other words, federal rules apply, but the school is required to enforce them.

Summary

The Perkins Loan program is an excellent source of low

interest money. The current interest rate is five percent with the availability of a repayment schedule spanning 10 years. A $30 minimum payment per month is usually required. Financial aid administrators often rely on the Perkins Loan program to supplement other federal and non-federal sources of funds when developing financial aid packages.

Examples of Perkins Loan Repayment Schedules (@ 5% interest):

Amount Borrowed	No. of Months	Monthly Payment
$ 1,000	36	$ 30.00
5,000	120	53.03
9,000	120	95.46
12,000	120	127.28
18,000	120	190.92

Chapter 15

College Work Study (CWS)

Learn and Earn at the Same Time.

That's one way to describe the College Work Study program. The CWS program provides students with jobs in order to earn money for school expenses. Both on-campus and off-campus jobs are supported by this federally subsidized program.

Does this Mean You Might Be Working for the Town's Tost Popular Video and Record Store?

No. A CWS job must always be for a public or private non-profit organization. Furthermore, if it's an off-campus job, there is another stipulation. The job must be in the public interest. Examples of such employers are federal, state or local public agencies.

Employers who hire CWS students are subsidized by the federal government. The federal government pays 80 percent of your wages, the remaining 20 percent is paid by your employer.

Both undergraduate and graduate students may apply for CWS jobs as long as their schools participate in this campus-based program. All applicants, however, must prove financial need. In other words, this program is a need-based program managed by the school's financial aid administrator.

How Much Can I Earn from the CWS Job?

The hourly rate will be at least the current federal minimum wage. Other factors can also influence the pay rate. For example the type of work you do and its difficulty both establish the value of a job.

Limitations

There are some limitations to the number of hours you may work. In some ways a CWS job may resemble a Pell Grant or a SEOG. Participants in the CWS program are awarded a specific amount of money. But unlike a grant, they must work at a job in order to get these funds. They, in effect, are earning the award over time.

So where's the resemblance? To begin with, a student can only earn a specific amount of money. For example, your CWS job may be good for $2,000. Even if you were willing to work double the hours required, additional funds could not be awarded to you. The federal government allocates money to each participating school for the CWS program. This money must then be divided among all qualified applicants.

Note that we used the term"qualified". That's another way the CWS program resembles grants. The amount you are allowed to earn is based on the following criteria:

1. Financial need.

2. Availability of funds earmarked for the CWS program at the school you are attending.

3. The amount of any other financial aid you are receiving.

Now you know why we say there are similarities among the programs. Furthermore, the amount allocated to each student in the program can vary from year to year. Not only do personal finances influence such allocations, but also the number of program applicants and the availability of federal funds.

Other considerations also come into play when awarding CWS jobs. Your class schedule, health, and academic progress are all reviewed. The school then tries to establish a compatible work schedule. For example, if you have morning classes it wouldn't be wise for the school's financial aid office to also arrange a morning job.

When Should I Apply For A CWS Job?

Most schools require you to apply early each calendar year. Different schools, however, have different deadlines. Talk with your school's financial aid administrator about school policy. As with any other program, apply as soon as possible so that you'll avoid the last-minute rush. Your award may also be affected by late application. Remember, only a limited amount of funds are available for the school. When these funds are gone, they're gone until next year!

CWS jobs are not automatically renewable. You must reapply each year just as you would for the other "need-based' programs we've described.

How Are CWS Students Paid?

Undergraduate students are paid by the hour. Graduate students may be paid either by the hour or salary. CWS students cannot be paid by commission or fee. In accordance with federal guidelines governing this program, participating schools must pay students at least once a month.

What If You're Not A Full-Time Student?

Depending on where you attend school, full-time status may not be an eligibility requirement for a CWS job. It's up to the school. For example, some schools allocate 10 percent of their CWS funds to part-time students. Check with your school's financial aid office for an explanation of their policy.

Summary

The CWS program is a great way for students to earn money for their education. Students qualifying for CWS jobs are informed by their schools in writing. The hourly wage or salary (salary is possible in the case of graduate students), is listed along with the total amount which can be earned for the current academic year. Some information about the employer is usually supplied. The letter may also contain information about other types of financial aid which has been arranged.

CWS jobs, like other student aid programs, are often mixed with other forms of financial aid in order to meet education expenses adequately. These financial aid packages may contain Pell Grant, GSL and/or scholarship monies.

Money Sources Worth Exploring

Persistence and creativity go a long way when it comes to financing a postsecondary education. There are many good sources of financial aid awaiting discovery by each year's roster of students.

In preceding chapters we concentrated on the better known financial aid programs. Are they the only source of money? No. As we said in our Introduction, everything from brains to athletic ability can qualify you for financial support. In fact, you don't even have to be blessed with any special talents. Your religious denomination or the company your father works for may be all it takes to obtain some much-needed funds.

We don't intend to present you with an in-depth analysis of what's available. That alone could fill an entire book. Our purpose is to get you thinking and asking questions. Check with your high school counselor or financial aid administrator for more detailed explanations. Your local library is another good source of information.

Start early when it comes to financial planning and searching to fund your postsecondary education. Don't be afraid to ask questions. Explore every opportunity that comes your way.

Cooperative Education

The Cooperative Education Program is often referred to as a "co-op" for short. It is a program that combines formal studies with an off-campus job. The job is related to your major. Money earned from the co-op job usually covers most if not all of your college expenses. More than 900 postsecondary schools participate in this program with an estimated 50,000 employers.

Usually one of the following methods is used for dividing a participating student's time between school and work:

1. Alternating Method: You rotate between being a full-time student for a term or semester and being a full-time employee for the alternate periods. This rotation cycle repeats itself until you graduate.

2. Parallel Method: You attend classes part-time and work between 15 and 25 hours per week.

3. Extended Day Method: You work full-time during the day and then attend classes in the evening.

All of these methods will more than likely result in your spending more time to obtain an undergraduate degree or complete your technical training. Keep in mind that although more time is required, you are basically paying for an education as you go rather than having to face a sizable debt upon graduation. A real bonus is that you may be working in your field of study, and this practical experience will make much of your classwork easier. Your employer, too, will see the development of a motivated, educated individual. Many companies have programs which reward these co-op students with promotions to higher skilled positions as soon as their schooling is completed.

For more information on this program, write:

National Commission for Cooperative Education
360 Huntington Avenue
Boston, MA 02115

Junior Fellowships

The Junior Fellowship Program is sponsored by the federal government. Students who rank in the upper 10 percent of their high school class and have financial needs may qualify for employment with a federal agency. Such jobs will be available during academic breaks.

Students participating in this program can currently earn between $8,000 and $10,000 during the four years it usually takes to earn an undergraduate degree. This program supports 5,000 fellowships. Application and selection for these openings are made during your senior year in high school.

Military

Local recruiters can help guide you through the maze of military-backed support for a postsecondary education. Financial support can be obtained before entering the service, while in uniform, and after being discharged. If either or both of your parents have served in the military, you may qualify for some forms of aid.

Health Professions Scholarship Programs:

Air Force:
Health Professions Recruiting
Building 1413, Stop 44
Andrews Air Force Base, MD 20331

Army:
Student Programs Management
Department of the Army (SGPE-PDM)
1900 Half Street, N.W.
Washington, DC 20324

Navy and Marines:
Bureau of Medicine and Surgery
(MED-214)
Navy Department
Washington, D.D. 20372

Military Academy Programs:

Air Force:
Director of Cadet Admissions
Air Force Academy
Colorado Springs, CO 80840

Army:
Admissions Office
U.S. Military Academy
West Point, NY 10096

Navy:
U.S. Naval Academy
Candidate Guidance Office
Annapolis, MD 21402

Coast Guard:
Director of Admissions
U.S. Coast Guard Academy
New London, CT 06320

Merchant Marine
Admissions Office
U.S. Merchant Marine Academy
Kings Point, NY 11024

Men and women who are United States citizens and who are between the ages of 17 and 25 can apply for the ROTC scholarship program. This program has both physical as well as academic requirements.

ROTC scholarships pay for tuition, books, and laboratory fees. They also provide monthly stipends for miscellaneous expenses. There is, however, a commitment the student must make. ROTC scholarship recipients must enlist in the Army, Navy, or Air Force while in college. Furthermore, the program requires a term of active duty military service after graduation. More than 600 postsecondary schools participate in the ROTC program nationwide.

ROTC Programs:
More information about the ROTC program can be obtained by writing:

Air Force:
Air Force ROTC
Office of Public Affairs
Maxwell AFB, AL 36112

Army:
Army ROTC Scholarship Program
Fort Monroe, VA 23651

Navy and Marines:
NROTC Scholarship Programs
4015 Wilson Blvd.
Arlington, VA 22203

Were members of your immediate family in the military? If the answer is "yes", then you might very well be eligible for special scholarships or interest-free loans. For a comprehensive list of these programs, order the following booklet from the American Legion. The cost is $1 per copy.

Need A Lift?
American Legion
P.O. Box 1055
Indianapolis, IN 46206

Both the Veterans Administration and the Social Security Administration support financial aid programs for postsecondary educations. Along with veterans, children of deceased, disabled, or retired veterans may also be eligible for benefits if they are covered under the Social Security Act. For more information, write:

Division of Student Services and Veterans Programs
400 Maryland Avenue, S.W.
Room 400
Washington, DC 20202

Female Students

When it comes to student aid programs, your sex can definitely make a difference. There are special assistance programs for female students. Information about some of the more active programs can be obtained by writing:

American Association of University Women
Educational Foundation Programs Office
2401 Virginia Avenue, N.W.
Washington, DC 20037

Business and Professional Women's Foundation
2021 Massachusetts Avenue, N.W.
Washington, DC 20036

National Association of Bank Women Scholarship
500 N. Michigan Avenue, Suite 1400
Chicago, IL 60611

Ethnic/Minority Students

Many ethnic and minority organizations support financial aid programs. For details about some of the more active ones write:

United Negro College Fund
500 East 62nd Street
New York, NY 10021

Roy Wilkins Educational Scholarship Program
NAACP
Youth and College Division
1790 Broadway
New York, NY 10019
National Hispanic Scholarship Fund
P.O.Box 748
San Francisco, CA 94101

National Hispanic Scholarship Awards Program
The College Board
888 Seventh Avenue
New York, NY 10126

Bureau of Indian Affairs
P.O. Box 15740
Sacramento, CA 95813

Japanese American Citizens League
Scholarship Committee
1765 Sutter Street
San Francisco, CA 94115

UNICO National (for Italian-Americans)
72 Burroughs Place
Bloomfield, NJ 07003

Kosciuszko Foundation (for Polish-Americans)
15 East 65th Street
New York, NY 10021

Daughters of Penelope (for Greek-Americans)
Scholarship Committee
Grand Lodge
1422 K Street, N.W.
Washington, DC 20005

Handicapped

Handicapped students may qualify for special assistance. For details write:

Clearinghouse for the Handicapped
South Portal Building, Room 3380
Washington, DC 20201

Alexander Graham Bell Association for the Deaf
3417 Volta Place, N.W.
Washington, DC 20007

Epilepsy Foundation of America
1828 L Street, N.W.
Washington, DC 20036

National Association, the Deaf-Blind of America
616 East 124th Street
Cleveland, OH 44108

Religious Denomination

Your religious denomination can qualify you for certain scholarships and/or low-interest loans. Talk with your clergyman about such a possibility. Most denominations do sponsor such programs on a national association basis, particularly in large metropolitan areas.

Intelligence and Talent

An excellent academic record is still one of the best and surest tickets to scholarship money. These "brain" awards are offered by the federal, state, and local governments, and private sponsors. Realize, however, that good grades are not always the only qualifying criteria. Financial need is often a consideration, as well as your selection of a field of study.

Do you have to be a "straight A" student to qualify for the academic awards?

Not always. Many of these awards are based on excellence in a particular field. For example, talent in music or dance, art, creative writing, leadership ability, and science or math aptitude are other examples of where special talent may win you financial support.

Do you have an unusual hobby or skill. Perhaps you're a rodeo champion or a chess enthusiast. Maybe you can build boats inside of bottles. Our point is that scholarship sponsors have a wide range of interest. Like the proverb, "seek and ye shall find", you too may find a surprising number of financial opportunities ... but only if you look for them.

So, where can you find these sponsors?

Talk with your high school counselor or financial aid administrator. Check with the public library for a copy of "Advisory List of National Contests and Activities". Copies of this publication may also be obtained by writing:

National Association of Secondary School Principals
1904 Association Drive
Reston, VA 22091

Another good strategy is to write any association related to the field you are pursuing. If they do not sponsor scholarships themselves, such associations can usually refer you to an organization that does.

Athletics

Are football heroes the only athletes who win scholarship money? Definitely not! In fact, the words "football" and "heroes" are both misleading.

First, let's take a look at what a wide range of sports can qualify you for financial aid. Along with football, there are baseball, basketball, hockey, soccer, track, sailing, badminton, tennis, gymnastics, lacrosse, bowling, archery, fencing, rowing, swimming, diving, skiing, and volleyball. There are others; we've just listed the better known sports. That's quite a selection!

Most colleges support financial aid programs for athletics. Sports is actually big business at many colleges and universities. The community, alumni, and students enjoy the team spirit and enthusiasm that sports events generate.

To qualify for such monies you have to be good but not fantastic. In other words, you have to be better than average but not necessarily great. Of course, the bigger name the school is, the more competition there's going to be for these dollars.

Draft a letter to the applicable coach at each school you are interested in. Tell the coach about both your academic interests and athletic achievements. If you've made the local sports page, include copies of these clippings. Ask the coach to explain any possibilities of financial aid and how to apply. Your high school coach should be able to lend some assistance.

For helpful booklets write:

The NCAA Guide for the College-Bound Student
NCAA Publishing
P.O. Box 1906
Shawnee Mission, KS 66222

High School Brochure
AIAW Publications
1201 16th Street, N.W.
Washington, DC 20036

Career Choice

Your career choice can open up many doors to financial aid. People in many careers belong to national organizations. These national organizations, in turn, often sponsor scholarships for promising students who desire to enter the profession.

Talk with people already working in the profession you are interested in. Ask them about regional and national associations they may be affiliated with. Write these associations asking about student aid programs. Again, your high school counselor or financial aid administrator can be of assistance. Another possible source of information is the public library. Most libraries have directories of national associations.

Clubs

The clubs you belong to may sponsor scholarships and/or low-interest loans. Write the home office of any club you are affiliated with, asking whether money is available for postsecondary education support. For example, if you belong to the Boy Scouts, write:

Education Relationship Services
Boy Scouts of America
1325 Walnut Hill Lane
Irving, TX 75038

Community

Civic associations, social clubs, professional groups, patriotic organizations, and other such groups in your own community may offer financial assistance to students. The Chamber of Commerce is a good source of such information. Also, look up "associations" in the Yellow Pages of your local telephone directory and call them.

Parents

Various aspects of your parents' lives may qualify you for financial assistance. Membership in a union, trade association, or fraternal association are common examples. Employers sometimes offer assistance to children of their employees.

Summary

There are countless sources worth exploring when it comes to financing a postsecondary education. Start early, be creative, don't be discouraged, and the odds are you'll be a winner in the race for college dollars!

Chapter 17

Why Plan for the Future?

In order for us to succeed at anything we do, we must have a plan. Any plan, no matter how simple it is, can serve as a useful guide for completion of the task at hand. A financial plan is no different. It serves as a map to help you plan for your financial future.

Each of us has a great deal of control over our future and that of our families. You are interested in your future or that of your children or grandchildren, or you wouldn't be reading this book. We want your future to be secure and certain, and we want to help limit financial uncertainties. How perfectly normal it is to want your children to have a better future than you might have had!

One means of providing for the future is to plan for the uncertainties that we all must face. That sounds simple. Take a few moments to think what each of us can do to ensure:

That basic needs of the family are met;
That there is protection against financial emergencies;
That adequate education needs are met;
A sufficient retirement program exists;
That the value of your estate is protected;
That the best tax strategy is employed, and;
That your investment plan is sound.

These seven programs can be managed by a carefully prepared and ongoing financial plan. Financial plans may be very simple and straightforward, or they may be complex documents prepared by a certified financial planner. These complex plans may be detailed documents over 100 pages long. The International Association for Financial Planning (IAFP) is an organization which represents over 17,000 professionals. Also, check with your bank, investment, or insurance firm to see if they have licensed and specially trained individuals who offer financial planning services.

Who needs a financial plan? The answer may surprise you. All of us do. For different reason at different times all of us need to prepare and follow a financial plan. Obviously one important group are those who have children contemplating postgraduate education. Costs of education have been increasing at a rapid pace in recent years, with no reversal of this trend in sight.

For a child who is presently 10 years old, the expected costs for a four-year college education could be as much as $59,000 at a state school and $89,000 at a private institution. Even if a child is currently in his or her teens, the anticipated future costs could be from $37,000 to $55,000. A financial plan is one means of analyzing your personal financial situation, earnings capacity, and amount of assets to determine if there are weaknesses in the ability to reach the important financial goals.

We typically plan for different things throughout our lives. When young and just starting a family, you will be planning for the basic needs of a larger family unit. You may plan for the acquisition of that first home, automobile, or even a business. Certainly, this plan may change as you grow older and find that long-term goals have changed. For example, retirement and the protection of your estate for beneficiaries may be the crucial issues.

Those who are single parents find themselves an ever-growing segment of the population. The single parent's financial needs are unique and a financial plan is no less important and valuable for them. We have mentioned that the availability of low-cost and government-supported programs may continue to be limited, no matter what the family size or worth. Because of the possibility of future reductions, all persons should prepare a financial plan for the future. In our next chapter, we've provided some basic guidelines anyone can use for developing a financial plan.

Chapter 18

How to Develop Your Personal Financial Plan

The development process consists of several steps. The first is to gather information, next you must establish goals and finally employ your resources to meet those financial goals.

The information gathering process requires that you list the balances and amounts in all of the applicable financial categories. Two forms are commonly used for step one. They are the Net Worth Statement or Balance Sheet and the Cash Flow Statement, (in many ways this form resembles an income statement).

The Balance Sheet is a "picture" of your financial position at one specific time. You could complete a new Balance Sheet each day; many businesses do. However, since this statement is intended to be a reflection of your finances at one point in time it is not necessary to recalculate it daily, weekly or even monthly (unless significant changes have occurred). We suggest that you complete the Balance Sheet at the end of each month or year depending on your particular situation. In other words, the more frequently personal finances change, the more often this form should be updated.

Assets are the things that you own. The asset section is usually divided into two subsections. Cash and things that are easily converted to cash are in the first "liquid asset" section. Other assets that may not be easily sold are in the second "non-liquid" or rather "fixed" asset section.

Review the following sample asset section:

Balance Sheet

Name _____

Date _____

Assets

  Liquid

    Cash _____

    Checking _____

    Savings _____

    Investments _____

    Life Insurance (cash value) _____

  Total Liquid _____

  Non-Liquid (Fixed)

    Annuities _____

    Retirement _____

    Real Estate _____

    Net Business Value _____

    Autos _____

    Personal Prop _____

  Total Fixed _____

  Total Assets _____

Let's review some of the terms used here. Investments listed should be those which can be easily sold and converted into cash. U.S. savings bonds and stocks of a recognized company sold routinely at various stock exchanges should be listed in the Liquid section. Stocks of a closely held company may not be readily sold and should be listed only in the fixed assets section. Furthermore, stocks should be listed at their real "fair market" value. What you'd expect to actually receive if you sold them today. Do not overvalue them. This is a common mistake. Unfortunately, many people regard "value" as what they would take for a certain item. This may be more than the item is really worth on the market.

Cash value life insurance IS NOT the same as the face value. Cash value is the savings that have accumulated in the insurance policy. It is usually a fraction of the premiums paid and, in the early years of the policy, it is quite small. Annuities are contracts which provide for a series of payments, much like your regular income. They are a form of insurance payment, payable at retirement, maturity or upon the death of the owner. They typically have some cash surrender value, but this is not considered "liquid" since the surrender procedures are sometimes complex and time consuming.

When listing real estate and home value, be realistic. List these items at the market value (i.e., what they would sell for today). Net business value is the net worth for the business balance sheet. Make certain that the business's balance sheet is accurately and conservatively completed.

The second section of the balance sheet is the liability section. This is a listing of your debts.

Liabilities

Current

Charge Accounts _____

Taxes _____

Bank Loans _____

Mortgage _____

Education _____

Other Current _____

Total Current _____

Non-Current

Mortgage _____

Bank Loans _____

Other Long Term _____

Total Long Term _____

Total Liabilities _____

The final section called "Net Worth" is very important. You simply total the values listed for all of the assets and subtract the total of all liabilities. The net difference (assuming that your assets are greater than liabilities) is the net worth.

Net Worth is shown by this simple equation:

Total Assets — Total Liabilities = Net Worth

Certain rules are usually followed in listing the liabilities. First, the section is divided into current and non-current portions. This is not absolutely necessary but it can prove to be helpful to have the debts broken down in this fashion. The current debts included those that are to be repaid in full within the next few years as well as the current portions of long-term debts. As an example, if you have just obtained a four-year car loan, you would list the next year's payment total in the current portion and the remaining three years' payments in the non-current portion. Be sure to reduce the non-current portion by the current portion so that you don't total the same amount twice.

The next step is to prepare a cash flow statement. This statement simply is a listing of the sources and uses of your cash. The Cash Flow is a cumulative statement. This means that it covers an accumulation of entries over some period of time. It is best to prepare this statement with an entire year's entries. For a more streamlined approach you may want to prepare two or more months and average them.

Cash Flow Statement

Source of cash

Gross Salary _____

Spouse's Salary _____

Dividends _____

Interest _____

Capital Gains (Loss) _____

Gifts _____

Other _____

Total Sources _____

Use of Cash

Tax — Income _____

Property _____

Social Security _____

Food _____

Mortgage or rent _____

Utilities _____

Maintenance _____

Furnishings _____

Transportation

Gas _____

Loan Payments _____

Repairs _____

Misc _____

Insurance

    Auto _____

    Home _____

    Other _____

Medical _____

Clothing _____

Contributions _____

Recreation _____

Loan Payments _____

Charge Accounts _____

Other Loans _____

Savings _____

Retirement _____

Alimony/Child Support _____

Other _____

    Total Uses _____

You may need other categories. Just add those that are applicable and delete unnecessary expense categories. You can see that this is intended to be an all-inclusive listing of the uses of monthly resources. You may list unusual amount in the month that they occurred or average them over the 12 month period. A good example would be tax refunds, settlements, or gifts.

Again, as with the balance sheet, subtract the total uses of cash from the total sources. The result will be "disposable" or "discretionary" income. This figure is the most important part of the process. It is from this "discretionary" source that you will make investments or savings to meet the goals of your financial plan.

What are the goals? We know that one will be to help meet the costs of education. If you know what the actual college budget will be, then use that figure. If not, you may assume an approximate cost per year of $6,000 if public and $10,000 if private. Vocational and technical costs vary but should be between $2,000 and $4,000 per year (if housing costs are not a factor).

Now that you have the discretionary income calculated and

the goal established, you must decide how to meet the desired goal. The first step is to determine the number of whole months until the goal is due to be met. Divide the cost by those months to determine the amount needed each month and compare this with the average monthly discretionary income. Is the income enough to cover your goal? If not, you may have to plan to supplement your savings with credit. Or can you liquidate some of the current or fixed assets listed on the balance sheet? You should integrate all of your financial goals into one plan, so that you will be able to achieve other major goals such as purchase or replacement of an automobile.

A financial planner may suggest methods of utilizing your discretionary income and assets to your best advantage. The plan will be used as a budget. The major spending needs, whether they be for education, retirement, home acquisition or improvements, or any of the other seven items listed in Chapter 17—Why Plan For The Future will be part of the plan. When properly prepared and followed, the plan and budget process will guide you in selecting the means to meet your goals. You can have control over you and your family's future . . . if you plan for it!

Chapter 19

The Future of Financial Aid

During recent years, federal lawmakers have been placing greater emphasis on finding ways to reduce federal spending for all GSL programs, (Student Loan, Parent Loan, and Supplemental Loans).

We previously mentioned the Graham-Rudman legislation and its 1986-87 budget balancing effects. In addition to these changes, the Student Loan program periodically comes before Congress for renewal or reauthorization. When this happens, Congress usually takes the opportunity to make some changes in the program.

We have provided an up-to-date review of the changes Congress made in the 1986 Higher Education Act Amendments. These changes include new interest rates, deferment, disbursement instructions, loan consolidation and new more stringent qualification requirements. Many of these changes effect existing program participants as well as the new student. It is important that the student borrower keep informed of the changes to determine which may apply to them.

The decade of the 80s and beyond will undoubtedly see more measures aimed at reducing the federal deficit. The changes we have seen in the student aid programs reflect this concern. Many state programs will be reduced if that state is also facing a budget deficit, and many are.

What can the student and parent do? The most important step you can take is to plan ahead. If your children are now nearing their postgraduate years, make plans to utilize the resources available to our best advantage. Keep abreast of the changes. When Congress is in session, review the recommendations for new legislation. It may be helpful to contact your congressman or senator. Let them know of your needs and concerns.

We can't be certain what the future will bring. What seems likely is that more steps will be taken to reduce the federal government's participation in these programs. Where possible, the shift of interest costs, default guarantee, administration, and even collection of the defaulted loans is being shifted to the private sector. These reductions likely will make aid for many Americans more difficult to obtain, but not impossible.

Most people in the financial community anticipate that aid programs will continue to play major roles in America's pursuit of higher education. These programs have contributed significantly to the increasing number of students who are attending our colleges, universities, business schools, trade, and technical schools. Although features of these programs do change from time to time, we believe that Congress will continue to make provisions for those who seek more knowledge through higher education. It is one of the best investments we can make in the future of our country.

Appendices

GLOSSARY

Accrued Interest — Interest on a loan that accumulates and must be paid at a later date.

Assets — Anything owned. Examples are cash, real estate, and savings accounts.

Campus-Based Programs — Refers to federal financial aid programs which are administered by a school's financial aid administrator. Examples are Supplemental Educational Opportunity Grants and National Direct Student Loans.

Collateral — Property pledged to secure a loan. By security we mean that the property can be taken back by the lender, if necessary, to be sold to recover the balance owed on the loan.

Cost of Education — Also referred to as "cost of attendance". Amount it will costs a student to attend a particular school. Typically includes tuition, room and board, books, supplies, and miscellaneous expenses. Depending on the financial aid program, however, the cost of education may exclude or include certain expenses. Check with your school's financial aid administrator to determine the specific items included for each program in which you are interested.

Deferment — Payment of loan principal and interest may be postponed because the borrower meets specified conditions. While a GSL is in deferment status, the federal government continues to pay the in-school interest subsidy.

Dependent Student — A student who under federal criteria is considered to be dependent on the parents and/or guardians for financial support.

Eligible Borrower — One who meets current legal requirements for borrowing under the GSLP.

Expected Family Contribution (EFC) — Calculated according to a standard need analysis formula, this amount represents how much a family will be expected to pay towards their child's postsecondary education. The calculated contribution is based on family savings; parent's, student's, and/or spouse's income; non-taxable income sources; and assets. This amount is then reduced by such factors as the size of the family, the number of family members, etc.

Financial Aid Package — Refers to the total amount of financial aid a student receives. May include federal and non-federal aid (i.e. loans, grants, scholarships). Using available resources to develop such a package for each interested student is one of the major responsibilities of a school's financial aid administrator.

Financial Aid Transcript — Refers to a record of all federal aid a student has received. Must be updated annually. If you transfer and request financial aid at the new school, this document must be sent to that school.

Forbearance — An arrangement in which the lender may delay loan repayment because of financial hardship to the borrower. Interest on the loan may be collected, or added to the loan balance.

Grace Period — A period of time specified by federal legislation in which a GSLP borrower does not have to begin repayment. The grace period begins once a borrower graduates, withdraws from school or falls below half-time status. The in-school interest subsidy continues during the grace period.

Grants — Awards made for educational purposes which do not have to be paid back.

Guarantee Agency — A state or non-profit entity that administers the student loan insurance program in a state. Although the federal government established regulations affecting various aspects of GSLs (i.e. interest rates), guarantee agencies in each state are free to institute their own additional guidelines as long as they are within federal policy.

Half-Time — Refers to enrollment status in an academic institution. Is used as an eligibility requirement for the GSLP. The following guidelines usually apply:

1. Schools measuring progress by credit-hours and academic terms (semesters, trimesters or quarters) require at least six semester hours or quarter hours per term.
2. Schools measuring progress by credit hours but not using academic terms require at least 12 semester hours or 18 quarter hours per year.
3. Schools measuring progress by clock hours require at least 12 hour per week.

Independent Student — A student who under federal criteria is considered to be financial self-supporting. The student must not have for the previous eight quarters: been declared dependent on parent's income tax return, lived with parent for more than six consecutive weeks during the year, and not received more than $750 in parental assistance.

In-School Interest Subsidy — Federal government's payment of interest that accrues on a GSL during the time that a borrower is enrolled in a postsecondary institution on a half-time or more basis. Is also paid during the loan's grace period and during period of deferment. Student does not repay this subsidy.

Interest — Fee paid or money collected for loaning or borrowing money.

Loan — Borrowed money that must be paid back.

Loan Guarantee — Legal promise made by federal government or the guarantee agency for loan repayment. Lenders are promised reimbursement including interest of loans defaulted or uncollectable because of bankruptcy, death or disability.

Origination Fee — Fee that each student must pay in order to receive a loan. Helps to reduce federal costs associated with the GSLP. Is currently temporarily 5.5 percent of the face value of the loan. Normal fee is five percent.

Principal — Face value of a loan.

Promissory Note — A legal document signed by the borrower when a GSL is awarded. Specifies the statutory terms and conditions of the loan, repayment terms and obligation to use loan proceeds for educational purposes only.

Remaining Need — Difference between the total amount of a borrower's cost of education and the sum of other forms of student financial aid. A GSL may not exceed the borrower's remaining need.

Secondary Market — A means by which owners of loans may sell them to a third party. May be sold for face value or a negotiable price. Borrower may make payments to the actual purchaser or to a third party servicer.

Special Allowance — Monies paid by the federal government to lenders each quarter for active GSLs. Is a compensation to lenders for the difference between GSL interest rates and the current market rates.

Statement of Educational Purpose — A document that must be signed in order to receive federal student aid. An agreement by the student to use financial aid money only to meet educational expenses.

BIBLIOGRAPHY

Clohan, William C., Jr., Esquire, *Guaranteed Student Loan Program (GSLP) — Overview, History, Policy Issues and Recommendations for — Reauthorization,* Consumer Bankers Association, 1985.

Dennis, Marguerite J., *Mortgaged Futures,* Hope Press, 1986.

Guaranteed Student Loan Program (GSLP) Briefing Book, FY83, U.S. Dept. of Education, Div. of Policy and Program Development, Guaranteed — Student Loan Branch, Analysis Section.

Guaranteed Student Loan Program in West Virginia, Higher Education Assistance Foundation (HEAF), 1981.

Harvard Student Agencies, Inc., *Making It,* E.P. Dutton & Co., Inc., 1973.

Hemar Group — A Partnership in Guaranteeing the Future, Annual Report, 1984.

Hemar Group — The New Credit Marketplace, Annual Report, 1985.

Leider, Ann J. *College Loans From Uncle Sam,* Octameron Associates, 1986.

Leider, Ann J. and Robert. *Don't Miss Out — The Amibitious Student's Guide to Financial Aid,* Octameron Associates, 1986.

Leider, Robert, *Your Own Financial Aid Factory,* A Peterson's Guide/Octameron Publication, 1984.

Paying For My Education . . . How Much Should I Borrow?, Hemar, 1985.

The Pell Grant Formula, 1986-87, U.S. Department of Education, 1986.

PLUS Loans, HEAF, 1981.

Regulations — Guaranteed Student Loan Program, Federal Register, Vol. 44 No. 181; Monday Sept. 17, 1979.

Regulations — Guaranteed Student Loan Program, Federal Register, Tues. June 24, 1980.

Regulations — Guaranteed Student Loan Program, Federal Register, Wed. April 21, 1982.

Rupp, Richard H., *Getting Through College,* Paulist Press, 1984.

Sallie Mae, Annual Report, 1984.

Sallie Mae, Annual Report, 1985.

The Student Guide — Five Federal Financial Aid Programs '86-'87, U.S. Department of Education, 1986.

APPENDIX A —
STUDENT AID REPORT (SAR)

Once you get federal aid, can you automatically count on it each year you are enrolled in school?

No. In order to get federal aid, you must reapply each year. That's your personal responsibility.

Your school's financial aid office will probably specify which form should be used to make application. Along with this form, the GSL and PLUS programs require other forms since they are handled by private lenders.

One of the most common forms used to make application for federal aid is the U.S. Department of Education's "Application for Federal Student Aid" (AFSA). However some schools use non-federal forms such as California's "Student Aid Application for California" (SAAC).

When you are filling out a non-federal form, there should be a special box on the document for forwarding purposes. this box is usually located near the end of the form. Just check the box if you want this information forwarded to the federal processing center. Then you too will be considered for federal assistance.

There are two versions of the AFSA form. Each has a special mailing address for submission purposes and is color coded as follows:

> Green — For Dependent Students
> Federal Student Aid Programs
> P.O. Box 4120
> Iowa City, IA 52244

> Grey — For Independent Students
> Federal Student Aid Programs
> P.O.Box 4121
> Iowa City, IA 52244

Anytime you apply for federal aid, regardless of whether the AFSA form is used, you will receive a Student Aid Report (SAR). Your SAR should arrive four to six weeks after the application is mailed.

The SAR contains information which you have previously supplied on the application form. Pell Grant eligibility is based on this information. Examples of the latter are family income, assets, and liabilities. The SAR also includes information indicating whether you qualify for Pell Grant money.

If you need help on filing a federal application or on correcting a SAR, call:

Federal Student Aid Information Center
(301) 984-4070

The information center also provides these other services free of charge:

1. Checks the status of an application
2. Checks on a school's eligibility for federal programs
3. Explains eligibility requirements
4. Explains how awards are determined
5. Assists with payment problems
6. Explains verification process
7. Explains requirement for federal programs
8. Mails publications on federal programs

Calls may be made anytime between the hours of 9:00 a.m. and 5:30 p.m. (Eastern Standard Time), Monday through Friday. However, this is not a toll-free number nor should collect calls be make. If you want the information, you must bear the slight expense of the call to obtain it.

If your SAR needs any corrections or additions, the adjusted document must be mailed to:

Federal Student Aid Programs
P.O. Box 4126
Iowa City, IA 52244

To request a copy of your SAR to change the mailing address, write:

Federal Student Aid Programs
P.O. Box 4127
Iowa City, IA 52244

To determine whether your application has been processed, write:

Federal Student Aid Programs
P.O. Box 4128
Iowa City, IA 52244

Important Note — Anytime you are making a written request regarding a SAR, always include your full name, permanent address, social security number, date of birth, and signature. Also, please keep a copy of all correspondence sent to or received from the federal student aid programs or any other center. It is wise also, to keep a record of the names of any persons you phone at the respective centers.

Once you are satisfied with the SAR, it's time to forward the document to the financial aid office at the college or school you plan to attend. A photocopy of both sides of Part 1 (an Information Summary) of the SAR is the first document needed.

Once you finalize your choice, submit the entire SAR to that school's financial aid office. The financial aid officer will use the SAR to award Pell Grant money (if eligible) along with other forms of aid.

APPENDIX B — STATE BY STATE LIST OF GUARANTEED STUDENT LOAN PROGRAM SOURCES

State Scholarship and Grant Program Sources

State Scholarship and Grant Programs

Alaska Commission on Postsecondary Education
Pouch F.P.
Juneau, AK 99811
(907) 465-2962

Alabama Commission on Higher Education
Suite 221- One Court Square
Montgomery, AL 36197
(205) 269-2700

Arkansas Department of Higher Education
1301 West Seventh Street
Little Rock, AR 72201
(501) 371-1441

Arizona Commission for Postsecondary Education
1645 West Jefferson — Suite 127
Phoenix, AZ 85007
(602) 255-3109

Student Aid Commission
1410 Fifth Street
Sacramento, CA 95814
(916) 445-0880

Colorado Commission on Higher Education
Colorado Heritage Center
1300 Broadway — 2nd Floor
Denver, CO 80203
(303) 866-2748

Board of Higher Education
61 Woodland Street
Hartford, CT 06105
(203) 366-2618

Delaware Postsecondary Education Commission
Carvel State Office Building
820 North French St. — 4th Floor
Wilmington, DE 19801
(302) 571-3240

Florida Student Financial Assistance Commission
Department of Education — Knott Building
Tallahassee, FL 32999
(904) 488-6181

Georgia Student Finance Authority
2082 East Exchange Place
Suite 200
Tucker, GA 30084
(404) 493-5444

State Postsecondary Education Commission
2444 Dole Street — Room 214
Honolulu, HI 96822
(808) 948-8213

Iowa College Aid Commission
201 Jewett Building
9th and Brand Ave.
Des Moines, IA 50309
(515) 281-3501

Office of State Board of Education
650 West State Street
Room 307
Boise, ID 83720
(208) 334-2270

Illinois State Scholarship Commission
102 Wilmot Road
Deerfield, IL 60015
(312) 948-8550

State Student Assistance Commission of Indiana
219 North Senate Ave.
Indianapolis, IN 46202-3294
(317) 232-2351

Kansas Board of Regents
Suite 609 — Capitol Towers
400 W. 8th Street
Topeka, KS 66603
(913) 296-3517

Kentucky Higher Education Assistance Authority
1050 U.S. 127 South
Frankfort, KY 40601
(502) 564-7990

Governor's Special Commission on Educational Services
P.O. Box 44127
Baton Rouge, LA 70804
(504) 925-3630

Massachusetts Board of Regents of Higher Education
Scholarship Committee — 330 Stuart Street
Boston, MA 02116
(617) 727-9420

Maryland State Scholarship Board
2100 Guilford Avenue
Baltimore, MD 21218
(301) 659-6420

Department of Educational and Cultural Services
State House — Station #23
Augusta, ME 04333
(207) 289-2183

Michigan Department of Education
Post Office Box 30008
Lansing, MI 48909
(517) 373-3394

Higher Education Coordinating Board
Suite 400 — Capitol Square Building
550 Cedar Street
St. Paul, MN 55101
(612) 296-3974

Department of Higher Education
P.O. Box 1438
Jefferson City, MO 65102
(314) 751-3940

Mississippi Postsecondary Educational Financial
  Assistance Board
Post Office Box 2336
Jackson, MS 39225-2336
(601) 982-6168

Montana University System
33 South Last Chance Gulch
Helena, MT 59601
(406) 444-6570

North Carolina State Education Assistance Authority
Post Office Box 2688
Chapel Hill, NC 27515
(919) 549-8614

State Board of Higher Education
10th Floor — State Capitol
Bismarck, ND 58505
(701) 224-4114

Nebraska Coordinating Commission for
  Postsecondary Education
Box 95005 — 301 Centennial Mall South
Lincoln, NE 68509
(402) 471-2847

New Hampshire Postsecondary Education Commission
61 South Spring Street
Concord, NH 03301
(603) 271-2555

Department of Higher Education
Office of Student Assistance
4 Quakerbridge Plaza One40
Trenton, NJ 08625
(609) 292-4646

Board of Educational Finance
1068 Cerrillos Road
Sante Fe, NM 87503
(505) 827-8300

University of Nevada-Reno
Rm. 200 TSSC
Reno, NV 89557
(702) 784-4666

New York State Higher Education Service Corp.
99 Washington Avenue
Albany, NY 12255
(518) 474-5642

Ohio Board of Regents
3600 State Office Tower
30 East Broad Street
Columbus, OH 43215
(614) 466-7420

Oklahoma State Regents for Higher Education
500 Education Building — State Capitol
Oklahoma City, OK 73105
(405) 521-8262

Oregon State Scholarship Commission
1445 Willamette Street
Eugene, OR 97401
(503) 686-4166

Pennsylvania Higher Education Assistance Agency
Towne House — 660 Boas Street
Harrisburg, PA 17102
(717) 787-1937

Rhode Island Higher Education Assistance Authority
274 Weybosset Street
Providence, RI 02903
(401) 277-2050

South Carolina Tuition Grants Agency
411 Keenan Building
Columbia, SC 29211
(803) 758-7070

Department of Education and Cultural Affairs
Richard F. Kneip Bldg. — 700 N. Illinois St.
Pierre, SD 57501
(605) 773-3134

Tennessee Student Assistance Corporation
B-3 Capitol Towers — Suite 9
Nashville, TN 37219
(615) 741-1346

Coordinating Board Texas College and University System
P.O. Box 12788 — Capitol Station
Austin, TX 78711
(512) 475-8169

Utah State Board of Regents
3 Triad Center — Suite 550
Salt Lake City, UT 84180-1205
(801) 533-5617

State Council of Higher Education for Virginia
James Monroe Bldg. — 101 N. 14th St.
Richmond, VA 23219
(804) 225-2141

Virginia State Education Assistance Authority
6 North Sixth Street
Richmond, VA 23219
(804) 786-2035

Vermont Student Assistance Corporation
Champlain Mill
P.O. box 2000
Winooski, VT 05404
(802) 655-9602

Council For Postsecondary Education
908 East Fifth Avenue
Olympia, WA 98504
(206) 753-3571

State Scholarship & Grant Program
P.O. Box 7858
Masision, WI 53707
(608) 266-2868

West Virginian Board of Regents
P.O. Box 4007
Charleston, WV 25364
(304) 347-1211

Wyoming Community College Commission
2301 Central Ave.
Barrett Bldg. — 3rd Floor
Cheyenne, WY 82002
(307) 777-7763

University of Guam
Uog Station
Mangilao, Guam 96913
(671) 734-2921

Higher Education Loan Program
1030 15th Street N.W.
Suite 1050
Washington, DC 20005
(202) 289-4500

Department of Human Services
Office of Postsecondary education Research & A
1331 H Street NW Suite 600
Washington, DC 20005
(202) 727-3688

Higher Education Assistance Foundation
1600 American National Bank Building
Fifth and Minnesota Street
Saint Paul, MN 35101
(612) 227-7661

Council on Higher Education
Box F — UPR Station
San Juan, Puerto Rico 00931
(809) 751-5082/1136

Virgin Islands Board of Education
P.O. Box 11900
St. Thomas, VI 00801
(809) 774-4546

Guaranteed Student Loan Programs

Alaska Commission on Postsecondary Education
Pouch FP
Juneau, AK 99801
(907) 465-2962

Alabama Guaranteed Student Loan Program
One Court Square — Suite 221
Montgomery, AL 36197
(205) 269-2700

Student Loan Guaranteed Foundation of Arkansas
Suite 515 — 1515 West 7th Street
Little Rock, AR 72202
(501) 371-2634

State Scholarship & Grant Program
3030 N. Central Suite 1407
Phoenix, AZ 85012
(602) 252-5793

California Student Aid Commission
1410 Fifth Street
Sacramento, CA 95814
(916) 445-0880

Guaranteed Student Loan Program
11990 Grant
Suite 500
North Glenn, CO 80233
(303) 450-9333

Connecticut Student Loan Foundation
25 Pratt Street
Hartford, CT 06103
(203) 547-1510

Delaware Higher Education Loan PGM
c/o Brandywine College
Post Office Box 7139
Wilmington, DE 19803
(302) 478-3000 Ext. 21

Florida Student Financial Assistance Commission
Knott Building
Tallahassee, FL 32999
(904) 488-4095

Georgia Higher Education Assistance Corporation
2082 E. Exchange Place — Suite 200
Tucker, GA 30084
(404) 493-5468

Hawaii Educational Loan Program
United Student Aid Funds Inc.
1314 So. King St. — Suite 962
Honolulu, HI 96814
(808) 536-3731

Iowa College Aid Commission
9th and Grand Ave.
201 Jewett Building — Room 201
Des Moines, IA 50309
(515) 281-4890

Student Loan Fund of Idaho Inc. Processing Center
P.O. Box 730
Fruitland, ID 83619
(208) 452-4058

Illinois Guaranteed Loan Program
102 Wilmot Road
Deerfield, IL 60015
(312) 945-7040

State Student Assistance Commission of Indiana
964 North Pennsylvania Ave.
Indianapolis, IN 46204
(317) 232-2371

Guaranteed Student Loan Program
Suite 600
6800 College Blvd.
Topeka, KS 66211
(913) 345-1300

Kentucky Higher Education Assistance Authority
1050 U.S. 127 South
Frankfort, KY 40601
(502) 564-7990

Governor's Special Commission on Educational Services
P.O. Box 44127-Capitol Station
Baton Rouge, LA 70804
(504) 925-3630

Massachusetts Higher Education Assistance Corporation
330 Stuart Street
Boston, MA 02116
(617) 426-9796

Maryland Higher Education Loan Corporation
2100 Guilford Avenue
Baltimore, MD 21218
(301) 659-6555

State Department of Cultural Services
Station 23
Augusta, ME 04333
(207) 289-2183

Michigan Higher Education Assistance Authority
Box 30047
Lansing, MI 48909
(517) 373-0760

Higher Education Assistance Foundation
1600 American National Bank Building
Fifth and Minnesota Streets
St. Paul, MN 55101
(612) 227-7661

Missouri Department of Higher Education
P.O. Box 1438
Jefferson City, MO 65102
(314) 751-3940

Mississippi Guaranteed Student Loan Agency
3825 Ridgewood Road — P.O. Box 342
Jackson, MS 39205-2336
(601) 982-6663

Montana University System
33 South Last Chance Gulch
Helena, MT 59620
(406) 444-6594

North Carolina State Education Assistance Authority
Post Office Box 2688
Chapel Hill, NC 27515
(919) 549-8614

North Dakota Guaranteed Student Loan Program
Box 5509
Bismarck, ND 58501-5509
(701) 224-5600

Higher Education Assistance Foundation
Cornhusker Bank Building
Suite 304 — 11th and Cornhusker Highway
Lincoln, NE 68521
(402) 476-9129

New Hampshire Higher Education Assistance Foundation
44 Warren Street
Concord, NH 03301
(603) 225-6612

Department of Higher Education
Office of Student Financial Assistance
C.N. 543
Trenton, NJ 08625
(609) 292-3906

Student Loan Guarantee Corporation
2301 Yale N.E. Building F
Albuquerque, NM 87106
(505) 843-7010

Nevada Department of Education
400 West King Street
Carson City, NV 89710
(702) 885-5914

New York State Higher Education Services Corp.
99 Washington Avenue
Albany, NY 12255
(518) 473-1574

Ohio Student Loan Commission
P.O. Box 16610
Columbus, OH 43216
(614) 462-6549

Oklahoma State Regents for Higher Education
500 Education Building — State Capitol
Oklahoma City, OK 73105
(405) 521-8262

Oregon State Scholarship Commission
1445 Willamette Street
Eugene, OR 97401
(503) 686-3200

Pennsylvania Higher Education Assistance Agency
660 Boas Street — Towne House
Harrisburg, PA 17102
(717) 787-1932

Rhode Island Higher Education Assistance Authority
274 Weybosset Street
Providence, RI 02903
(401) 277-2050

South Carolina Student Loan Corporation
INterstate Center — Suite 210
P.O. Box 21487
Columbia, SC 29221
(803) 798-0916

South Dakota Education Assistance Corporation
115 First Avenue S.W.
Aberdeen, SD 57401
(605) 225-6423

Tennessee Student Assistance Corporation
B-3 Capitol Towers — Suite 9
Nashville, TN 37219
(615) 741-1346

Texas Guaranteed Student Loan Corp.
P.O. Box 15996
Austin, TX 78761
(512) 835-1900

Utah Education Loan Services
1706 Major St.
Salt Lake City, UT 84115
(801) 487-4448

Vermont Student Assistance Corporation
Champlain Mill
P.O. Box 2000
Winooski, VT 605404-2000
(802) 655-9602

Washington Student Loan Guaranty Assoc.
500 Colman Building
811 First Avenue South
Seattle, WA 98104
(206) 625-1030

Guaranteed Student Loan Program
Post Office Box 7860
Madison, WI 53707
(608) 246-1700

Higher Education Assistance Foundation
P.O. Box 591
Charleston, WV 25322
(304) 345-7211

Higher Education Assistance Foundation
American National Bank Building
Suite 320 — 20th at Capitol Avenue
Cheyenne, WY 82001
(307) 635-3259

Puerto Rico Higher Education Assistance Corporation
P.O. Box 42001 — Minillas Station
Santurce, Puerto Rico 00940-2001
(809) 726-2525

Student Loan Marketing Association
1055 Thomas Jefferson Street NW
Washington, DC 20002
(202) 333-8000

United Student Aid Funds Inc.
Processing Center
P.O. Box 50827
Indianapolis, IN 46250
(800) 428-9250

Virgin Islands Board of Education
P.O. Box 11900
St. Thomas, VI 00801
(809) 774-4546

APPENDIX C — STUDENT LOAN DEPARTMENT PAYMENT TABLE INSTRUCTIONS AND WORKSHEET

If you anticipate borrowing for your education in future years, you may estimate the amount you will owe at the conclusion of your education by multiplying the amount you borrowed this year by the number of years remaining in your educational program (not counting this year) and adding the result to your current outstanding indebtedness.

For example, if you borrowed $2,625 in GSLs this year and you have two years of school to complete after this year, you would multiply $2,625 by two for a total of $5,250 and $6,000 for a total indebtedness of $11,250 at the conclusion of your education. Part A of the Worksheet on page 153 is provided to assist you in projecting the amount you will owe at the conclusion of your education.

Use the Monthly Payment Table on page 152 and Part B of the Worksheet to calculate an estimate of your monthly payments. The monthly payment amounts are based on a repayment period of 10 years, which is the maximum allowable repayment period. If the repayment period on your loan is scheduled for less than 10 years, your monthly payments will be greater than those indicated on the Table. The table should be used as follows:

(1) For your GSLs, select the applicable interest rate column on the table (7, 8 or 9 percent), and locate your total cumulative outstanding loan balance figures in the left hand column on the table. If necessary, add two estimates of monthly payments together to most closely approximate your total monthly payment.

> **Example:** A borrower with $17,000 outstanding in 8 per cent GSLs would select the estimate of $121.33 for $10,000 of GSLs and $84.93 for $7,000 of GSLs, and add the two together for a total estimated monthly repayment of $206.26. This figure would be placed in Part B, column 1 of your worksheet.

(2) For any ALAS, PLUS, or Supplemental Student Loan, select the applicable interest rate column on the table (7, 8, 9, 10, 11, 12, or 14 percent) that amount closely approximates your current interest rate. For PLUS/ALAS loans made prior to October 17, 1986,the rate is either 12 or 14 percent. For

Supplemental Student Loans made with a variable rate (these may include refinanced PLUS or ALAS loans), select the rate that most closely approximates the current rate on the loan. The rate on these loans is subject to annual adjustment and thus monthly repayments cannot be estimated with great accuracy. Match up your total cumulative outstanding balance with the appropriate interest rate and cumulative outstanding balance figures. If necessary, add the estimates of monthly payments together to approximate most closely your total estimated monthly payments. This figure is placed in Part B, column 2 of your worksheet. The result of these calculations is an estimate based on the amount you are borrowing this year. You may borrow more or less,in future years depending on your circumstances. If so, your monthly payments will be different from this estimate.

> **Example:** A borrower has a total of $20,000 outstanding in PLUS/ALAS loans. Of this amount, $10,000 is for 14 percent ALAS loans. Another $10,000 are SLS loans made at a variable interest rate, which is presently set at 9.6 percent. For the 14 percent loans, the table indicates that the estimated monthly payment is $155.27. For the SLS loans, the current interest rate of 9.6 percent should be rounded to the nearest percentage rate and matched up with the appropriate column on the table. Using this column, for a cumulative outstanding balance of $10,000, the estimated monthly payment is $132.16. The sum of the two estimated monthly payments of $155.27 and $132.16, $287.43 is the total estimated monthly payment for this borrower's ALAS and SLS loans. (Part B, column 2 of the Worksheet.)

(3) Add together the total estimated monthly payments from columns 1 and 2. This is your total estimated monthly payment. This figure should be carefully considered in any future borrowing plans under the GSL, PLUS, or SLS loans programs.

MONTHLY PAYMENT TABLE

Total Balance	7%	8%	9%	10%	11%	12%	13%	14%
*$ 1,000	$ 11.62	$ 12.14	$ 12.67	$ 13.22	$ 13.78	$ 14.35	$ 14.94	$ 15.53
* 2,000	23.23	24.27	25.34	26.44	27.56	28.70	29.87	31.06
* 3,000	34.84	36.40	38.01	39.65	41.33	43.05	44.80	46.58
* 4,000	46.45	48.54	50.68	52.87	55.11	57.39	59.73	62.11
5,000	58.06	60.67	63.34	66.08	68.88	71.74	74.66	77.64
6,000	69.97	72.80	76.01	79.30	82.66	86.09	89.59	93.16
7,000	81.28	84.93	88.68	92.51	96.43	100.43	104.52	108.69
8,000	92.89	97.07	101.35	105.73	110.21	114.78	119.45	124.22
9,000	104.50	109.20	114.01	118.94	123.98	129.13	134.38	139.74
10,000	116.11	121.33	126.68	132.16	137.76	143.38	149.32	155.27
15,000	174.17	182.00	190.02	198.23	206.63	215.21	223.97	232.90
20,000	232.22	242.66	253.36	264.31	275.51	286.95	298.63	310.54
25,000	290.28	303.32	316.69	330.38	344.38	358.68	373.28	388.17
30,000	348.33	363.99	380,03	396.46	413.26	430.42	447.94	465.80
35,000	406.38	424.65	443.37	462.53	482.13	502.15	522.59	543.44
40,000	464.44	485.32	506.71	528.61	551.01	573.89	597.25	621.07
45,000	522.49	545.98	570.05	594.68	619.88	645.62	671.90	698.70
50,000	580.55	606.64	633.38	660.76	688.76	717.36	746.56	776.34

*If the total balance is $4,000 or less, monthly payments nevertheless must not be less than $50.

WORKSHEET

A. Projection of Indebtedness at Conclusion of Education

Amount Borrowed
this year
_____

× Years remaining in educational
program (exclude this year)
_____

= Estimate of
future borrowing
_____

Estimate of
future borrowing
_____

+ Current outstanding
indebtedness
(include this loan)
_____

= Estimated debt at conclusion
of Education
_____

B. Monthly Payment Calculation

Column 1
Monthly Payment GSLs
_____

+ Column 2
Monthly Payment on PLUS/
ALAS/SLS
_____

= Column 3
Total monthly Payment
_____

BLUE RIDGE BANK, NA
One Mountain Drive   Box 101
Park Hills, VA 25326

Dear Student Loan Customer:

Your Student Loan/Plus Loan/SLS check was mailed to the school today.

We want you to be aware of your rights and responsibilities relating to this loan. These were previously described for you in the promissory note you signed and in the materials you received with your application. If you need an additional copy of the disclosure form, please contact us.

Please remember this loan is your debt and must be repaid. If you leave school or cease to carry at least one-half academic workload, you must contact us immediately to set up repayment. You may be eligible to defer repayment of your loan under certain circumstances as described to you in your GSL material. You may prepay your loan at any time without penalty. You must keep us informed of changes in your address and enrollment status in school.

As a reminder, failure to repay your loan according to its terms and conditions will result in reporting your default to a credit bureau and may result in any or all of the following:

1. loss of Federal and/or State income tax refunds
2. legal action
3. loss of eligibility for Federal Student Aid
4. difficulty in obtaining other credit

If you have any questions, please contact the student loan department.

WE ARE PLEASED TO BE A PART OF EDUCATING
YOUNG AMERICANS.

Lana J. Chandler

A banking professional since 1974, Lana Chandler is Manager of Loan Systens for a major West Virginia bank. She is the author of four books, including *Putting Your Money to Work* (Betterway Publications, 1986), and a frequent articles contributor to banking, management, and data processing publications. Lana is a resident of Charleston, West Virginia.

Michael D. Boggs

A banking veteran of fourteen years, Mike Boggs is Managing Officer, Student Loan Services, for the same West Virginia bank. He is a part-time instructor in banking and finance at West Virginia State College, and has been active as an officer of the Charleston chapter of the American Institute of Banking for the past five years. Mike lives with his wife and their two daughters in St. Albans, West Virginia.

Index

(Pell Grant, continued)
ADS Student Report, 82
Alternate Disbursement System, (ADS), 83
application for, 81-2
application processing center, 81
applications, 96
dependent student formula, 85-6, 87-8
eligibility requirements, 95-6
federal student aid information center, 81
Formula Book, 77
independent student formula, 89-90, 91, 92-3
maximum award, 77-8
program funding, 82-3
qualifications, 77
SAI calculations, 79-80
Student Aid Index, (SAI), 77-8
Student Aid Report, (SAR), 81
tables, 84-93
Pell Grant Methodology, 77-8
Perkins Loan, 97-104
borrower responsibilities, 103
cancellation, 102-3
deferment, 101-2
eligibility requirements, 98-9
loan limits, 98
repayment, 97, 100-1
Perkins Loan Program, (formerly NDSL), 8
Personal financial plan, 121-6
Planning for the future, 119-20
PLUS, (Parent Loans for Undergraduate Students), 8, 33-8
Postsecondary education costs, 11-2
factors influencing, 20
Presidential Sequester Order, 64

R
Religious denominations, money sources for, 115
Repayment, 55-61
bankruptcy, 58
death or disability claims, 57-8
deferments, 58-60
forbearance, 58
grace period, 57
PLUS Program, 55
summary guidelines, 61
term of loan, 57
worksheets, 55-6
ROTC Programs, 112-3
Roy Wilkins Educational Scholarship Program, (NAACP), 114

S
SAI, Student Aid Index, 25-6
Sallie Mae, 71
Student Loan Marketing Association, 12

Scholarships, athletics, money sources of, 116-7
SEOG (Supplemental Education Opportunity Grant), 7
Service agencies, 71-3
function of, 71-2
SGA, State Guarantee Agencies, 16
SLS (Supplemental Loans for Students), 8
Social Security Administration, 113
Social Security educational benefits, 27
Special allowance fee, 64
State Guarantee Agencies, (SGA), 16, 28
State Student Loan Agencies, 16, 28
Statement of Educational Purpose, 24
defined, 132
Statement of Registration Status, (Selective Service), 23-4
Student Aid Index, (SAI), 25-6
Student Loan Marketing Association, (Sallie Mae), 12
Student loan repayment tables and worksheets, 150-4
Student Loan Report (SAR), 134-6
Student loans, 23-32
Supplemental Educational Opportunity Grant, (SEOG), 7, 95-6
Supplemental Loan Program, 39-43, 55
borrowing limits, 41
deferment, 43
eligibility requirements, 40-1
lending guidelines, 42
limitations, 39
repayment options, 41-2
Supplemental Loans for Students, (SLS), 8

T
Tax law revisions, 1986, 37
The NCAA Guide for the College-Bound Student, 117

U
U.S. Office of Education, 14
agency evaluation, 14
Division of Eligibility, 14
U.S. Savings Bonds, 38
UNICO National (for Italian-Americans), 114
United Negro College Fund, 114
United Student Aid Fund, (USAF), 16
Unusual talents, money sources for, 115-6
USAF, United Student Aid Fund, 16

V
Variable-rate loans, 64
Veterans Administration, 113
as source of financial aid, 8
Veterans Administration educational benefits, 27